A Tribute to Menno Simons

By Franklin H. Littell

Professor of Church History
Perkins School of Theology,
Southern Methodist University

HERALD PRESS, SCOTTDALE, PENNSYLVANIA

The Author

Franklin H. Littell is Professor of Church History at Perkins School of Theology, Southern Methodist University, Dallas, Texas. His Ph.D. degree was secured at Yale University with a dissertation on *The Anabaptist View of the Church,* which was published as a Brewer Prize book in 1952 (revised and enlarged in 1958). His writings include two other books in English, *The Free Church* (1957) and *The German Phoenix* (1960), in addition to numerous articles in scholarly journals. During nearly a decade in postwar Germany as a member of the Religious Affairs Staff (U.S.A.) and Director of the Franz Lieber Foundation he was closely related to the movement known as the Kirchentag as well as to the Evangelical Academies, and received the degree of Doctor of Theology *honoris causa* from the University of Marburg (1957). He is a widely used preacher and lecturer, and an ordained minister in the Methodist Church.

Printed in United States of America

Foreword

Four hundred years ago this year a humble and hunted pioneer of the Free Church way died a natural death, although for two decades he had moved secretly among the Dutch Anabaptist congregations with a heavy bounty offered by the Empire for his betrayal. Many of his colleagues in the movement were less fortunate and ended their days in the baptism of blood, by burning, drowning or beheading—for such was the price which Christendom exacted at that time from those who attempted to practice a church life based on voluntaryism and liberty of conscience.

In spite of the embarrassment which most descendants of the Protestant and Roman Catholic state churches now feel at being reminded of those cruel times, that feeling has rarely been acute enough to lead them to familiarize themselves with the actual testimony for which the Anabaptist/Mennonite martyrs died and for which Menno Simons (1496-1561) lived out his years. It has been my intention in this tribute volume, therefore, to give first attention to Menno's own writings. Enough books have been written, and are still being published, which treat Anabaptism and its leaders in defiance of the canons which normally obtain in the historical field: i.e., based solely on the oft-repeated charges of those who harrassed the little bands who were attempting a restitution of New Testament church life, and who harried their leaders in the conviction that religious dissent was civic disloyalty.

The Associated Mennonite Biblical Seminaries of Elkhart and Goshen, Indiana, generously extended to me the opportunity to pay this tribute—long intended, and matured during two decades of research and writing on Anabaptist, Mennonite and Free Church history—under their auspices and in their friendly atmosphere. I am mindful of the fact that this readiness to engage in dialogue with an out-grouper is an authentic expression of their own tradition, and that there are considerable sections of Christendom to this day which do not extend them the same Christian charity. This is, in the long, more impoverishing to a bruised and anxious Christendom than it is dismaying to a people who have through generations borne a calm and confident minority witness.

It will become evident, I trust, that Menno Simons has some important points to contribute to the present effort of the Christian churches to discover what God purposes with them in mid-twentieth century. Indeed, the most fitting tribute to his memory may be to make a small contribution to what was his own constant concern: that the Word which liberates and makes new should be proclaimed wherever there are ears to hear it.

Dallas, Texas   F. H. L.
March, 1961

Introduction

The quadricentennial of the death of Menno Simons January 29, 1961, has occasioned not only numerous appreciative commemorations but also a number of re-evaluations of his contribution as a reformer. The fresh look reveals a man who though not among the greatest of the Protestant leaders was nevertheless of substantial significance with a unique contribution. Without question he was the greatest all-round leader of the sixteenth-century Anabaptists, and his spiritual descendants in all branches of the Anabaptist-Mennonite movement have continued to profit from his clear and effective enunciation of the basic principles of the brotherhood when it was true to its foundational commitments.

But Menno's contribution is also to Protestantism in general. His voice was a unique one, for in the sixteenth century Anabaptism was a distinctive third type in the Reformation alongside of Lutheranism and Calvinism. But Menno also speaks in a strikingly relevant way to the issues which stir the modern church.

It is the merit of Franklin Littell's tribute to Menno to have demonstrated the relevance of Menno's thought for today in four of the major concerns which mark the current revival in Protestant theology: the Word of God; the True Church; the Role of the Laity in the Church; and the Doctrine of the Holy Spirit.

The four chapters of this book were delivered as the Annual Seminary Lectureship of the Associated Mennonite Biblical Seminaries at Elkhart, Indiana, in March 1961 under the general title: "The Theology of Menno Simons and Its Significance for Today." The Mennonite Biblical Seminary at Elkhart and the Goshen College Biblical Seminary at Goshen, Indiana, as joint sponsors of the Lectureship, are happy to release the lectures for publication by the Herald Press under the book title, *A Tribute to Menno Simons.*

May 1961   Harold S. Bender, for the Associated
                          Mennonite Biblical Seminaries

Table of Contents

Foreword   5

Introduction   6

Chapter   I—MENNO AND THE WORD OF GOD   9

Chapter   II—MENNO AND THE TRUE CHURCH   23

Chapter III—MENNO AND THE DOCTRINE OF THE LAITY   37

Chapter IV—MENNO AND THE DOCTRINE OF THE HOLY SPIRIT 53

Footnotes   69

Menno and the Word of God

In the current ecumenical debate we often hear the assertion that the course of theology in the last generation has been one of rediscovery. In the use of the word "rediscovery" there is implicit, of course, the admission of a certain blindness in the past. And now, it is said, the scales have been removed from the eyes and those truths which were neglected have again come to receive central attention. Thus Dr. W. A. Visser't Hooft, speaking at the meeting in Hannover in 1949 which founded the great rally of the church, the *Deutscher Evangelischer Kirchentag*, used these words:

The sign of real life in the European churches, especially during the war, is *the return to the Bible* as the source of all knowledge.[1]

We are told that Christendom, burdened by the shame of its own apostasy during the easy decades of the nineteenth century and shocked by the upsurge of demonic secular religions in the twentieth century, has turned its eyes again toward the rallying points of Christian intellectual discipline. First there was the rediscovery of the Bible. This was symbolized perhaps by Karl Barth's *Commentary on Romans* (1919, 1922) and drawn to a climax in the Barmen Deolaration (May, 1934), in which all supposed revelations apart from the one Word of God were resolutely repudiated.

We repudiate the false teaching that the church can and must recognize yet other happenings and powers, images and truths as divine revelation alongside this one Word of God, as a source of her preaching.[2]

2

There followed after the rediscovery of the church. This might be symbolized most readily perhaps by reference to Dietrich Bonhoeffer's *Sanctorum Communio,* in which he wrote of the whole theological enterprise:

It would be good to begin a dogmatic treatise for once not with the doctrine of God but with the doctrine of the church, in order to make clear the inner logic of dogmatic construction.[3]

After this came the rediscovery of the laity. The author of the leading book on this area of ecumenical concern is the great missionary theologian, Professor Hendrik Kraemer, founder of the lay institute "Kerk en Wereld." In his book, *A Theology of the Laity,* we read:

The laity or the body of lay-membership of the church has never in church history enjoyed the distinction of being treated with care and thoroughness as a matter of specific theological importance or significance.[4]

Last of all, and just coming into focus with the international conference at Lund (1952), is the truth contained in the doctrine of the Holy Spirit.

The purpose of these lectures is not to determine whether or not it is true that the Bible, the church, the laity, and the Holy Spirit have in fact been "rediscovered." It is enough for our purposes that much of contemporary Christian thinking has this image of recent church history. These lectures, the tribute of an out-grouper to the heritage of Menno Simons, are intended to reveal what the teachings of Menno Simons have to contribute to those who want to take Bible, church, laity, and Holy Spirit seriously as foci of Christian creed and confession.

In his *Confession of the Triune God* (1550), Menno stated his stand in reference to the Word of God.

Brethren, as for me, I confess that I would rather die than to believe and teach my brethren a single word or letter concerning the Father, the Son, and the Holy Ghost (before God I lie not) contrary to the plain testimony of the Word of God which so clearly points out and teaches through the prophets, evangelists, and apostles. . . .

I know very certainly that if any one wants to go further than we testify and admonish here from the Word of God, he will lose his way, mount too high, deviate to one side. He will miss the road and will act no more intelligently than he who would try to pour the river Rhine or Meuse into a quart bottle. But those who abide simply and humbly by the Word of God . . . and firmly believe it, although they do not and cannot fully comprehend it; and guard against all human investigation, disputations, glosses, explanations, perversions, and conjecture in these incomprehensible depths; these will in all temptations stand firmly by the grace of God, and walk all their lives before their God with calm, glad hearts.[5]

Here two characteristic notes stand out: First, Menno purposes that the Word is the standard by which doctrinal instruction is to be tested and checked: his creed is the Bible itself. Second, the Christian is to avoid speculation: the adding of glosses, explanations, and conjecture can but bring confusion and generate pride. In rebuking John a Lasco's approach he commented:

Philosophy, rationalization, and glosses, we shall, I greatly fear, have a plenty, but very little of the power of Scripture, its basis and truth.[6]

In the *Foundation of Christian Doctrine* (1539), he was equally explicit.

This command and word, I say, Christ commanded all true messengers and preachers to observe, saying, Preach the gospel. He does not say, Preach the doctrines and commands of men, preach councils and customs, preach glosses and opinions of the learned. He says, Preach the gospel. Teaching them to observe all things whatsoever I have commanded you. Matt. 28:20.[7]

His attitude in this matter is the same as his attitude to the reform of the corrupted church. In both cases it is the addition of unnecessary and undesirable increment which has produced a "fall," in one case in Christian thought, in the other case in the structure and style of the institution itself.

The true evangelical faith sees and considers only the doctrine, ceremonies, commands, prohibitions, and the perfect example of Christ, and strives to conform thereto with all its power.[8]

11

In both cases the solution is to return to a direct encounter with the Word of God and its claims upon us. This is very close to the emphasis of Karl Barth in the *Commentary on Romans:* The Scripture is itself the sovereign and self-revealing Word of God. In the words of another crisis theologian, we are to "read the Bible until it reads to us." It is the very human desire to use the Bible to justify our own ideas, our own purposes, our own way of life, which leads to additions, amendments, deletions, which corrupts. The initiative must remain with the Word of God, which judges or redeems in terms of where we stand in relationship to "it." (The Word is not really "it," neuter gender, although at this moment the quality of simple objectivity may best be asserted in that form.)

The Bible, then, "speaks" to the church. Those who hear and obey are formed by this action. The Word is to be conceived in the totality of its intent and impact, not used for picking and choosing. The old covenant, although superseded in part in morals and cultic rites, is still the first book of Christian history. There is no place for anti-Semitism in Anabaptism. As was later to be said in rebuke to Hitler, we are all "spiritual Semites." Here again the contrast of Menno and Luther is striking!

Menno protested the very common abuse of breaking the unity of the Bible, proof-texting, of using a few words or phrases out of context to prove something contrary to the spirit and intent of the total Biblical revelation. Writing in *Christian Baptism* (1539), he commented that

> . . . it is the nature of all heresies to tear a fragment from the holy Scriptures and thereby to defend their adopted worship. They do not regard that which is written before or after, by which we may ascertain the right meaning. . . .[9]

It is the whole intent of the whole Gospel which must command us, not some tiny portion lifted out to suit our own inclinations. "Word of Christ," "Word of God," "holy Scriptures," "the word of the Lord"—are used interchangeably by Menno. It is the whole revelatory word of the Bible which is proclaimed, to be taken seriously, and Menno does not hesitate to criticize reformers, popes, or church fathers where they have strayed from the "clear, chaste, and plain doctrine of Christ Jesus."[10] "Only show us the Word of God, and the matter is settled."[11] And, as deeply as he desired the baptism of the converted, he did not slip into a magical view of the rite: "We are not cleansed by the washing of the water, but by the Word of the Lord. . . ."[12]

Just as dangerous as the glosses and speculations of the philosophers and canon-lawyers are the visions and special revelations of the prophets. At this point Menno was most insistent, for he was gathering up some of the faithful from persons who had temporarily been led away by religious revolutionaries like John of Leiden and spiritualist visionaries like David Joris. In his first book, on the *Blasphemy of John of Leiden* (1535), he condemned the false teachers who "traffic in strange doctrine."

Let every one of you guard against all strange doctrine of swords and resistance and other like things which is nothing short of a fair flower under which lies hidden an evil serpent which has shot his venom into many. Let everyone beware.[13]

In his warning "To the Corrupt Sects," Menno asked the telling question to be directed to all claiming a fuller knowledge, a more perfect revelation:

Do you mean to say that the doctrine of Christ and His apostles was incomplete and that your teachers bring forth the perfect instruction?[14]

Here again we are reminded of Barmen, of the answer to special revelations in the twentieth century, as well as of the stand of the early church against the Gnostic heresies.

I would then herewith sincerely admonish you all to weigh and prove all spirits, doctrine, faith, and conduct with the Spirit of Christ; and that ye be sane.[15]

Against visionaries he wrote with special fervor, for the sixteenth century ferment produced a host of them, and the state churches' neglect of the common folk led many to turn to inspired prophets. He insisted that he was not speaking "by some revelation or heavenly inspiration, but by the express, definite Word of the Lord."

> I am no Enoch, I am no Elias, I am not one who sees visions, I am no prophet who can teach and prophesy otherwise than what is written in the Word of God and understood in the Spirit . . . . Once more, I have no visions nor angelic inspirations. Neither do I desire such lest I be deceived. The Word of Christ alone is sufficient for me.[16]

Such is the corruption and downward bent of the world, however, that "from the beginning of the world genuine righteousness and devout piety have been in this way miserably hated, persecuted, cast out and killed. . . ." He attributed the persecution which the princes and rulers of the world brought against him and his flock to their holding to the rule of Christ.

> . . . because we judge and try all spirits, doctrines, counsels, ordinances, statutes, and ceremonies, in so far as they concern the spirit and the faith, with the Spirit, the doctrine, the ordinances, and the commandments of Christ. . . .[17]
> O Lord, with that unjust hatred they hate me; whom have I wronged in a single word? Whom have I shortchanged a penny's worth? Whose gold, silver, cow or cattle, ox or ass have I desired? I have loved them with a pure love, even unto death; Thy word and will have I taught them, and with earnest diligence I have shown them by Thy grace the way of salvation. Therefore my enemies are so many, and hate me with cruel hatred.[18]

In short, the Word defined both the church and the world: what accepted and was made new was "church." What resisted, hated, turned to violence of rejection, was "world."

The church numbered, in visible and covenanted assembly, those who had ears to hear, who turned again, who awoke to believe. She numbered also those faithful of the past and future..

Ours is no new doctrine, as the preachers without truth assert

14

and would have you believe. It is the old doctrine which was preached and practiced in the church for more than 1,500 years, the doctrine by which the church was begotten, is being begotten, and will be begotten to the end.[19]

It was the living Word, planted in the midst of the faithful, which created the church. Here the "it" of neuter gender, used to refer to the objective validity of the Word—its *selbstbezeugende* character—becomes the deeply personal and interacting. The initiative lies in the Word, which was in the beginning; but in penetrating men's lives "it" becomes deeply personal and the action can only be associated with the personal pronoun, "He."

It is precisely at this point that we find one of the most significant aspects of Menno's theology. For the person acting is not described in terms of the second person of the Christian Trinity: He is God the Holy Spirit, creating, governing, sending, sanctifying. The significance of this doctrinal emphasis, in a Protestantism large sections of which have neglected the doctrine of the third person and sentimentalized the doctrine of the second person, will receive fuller treatment later. For the present it is important to point out the significance of this turning point for the understanding of the Word of God.

The Word which creates the church and is the "food of the regenerate"[20] is also *verbum peregrinatum*. The mobility of the early Anabaptist-Mennonite preachers was by no means due primarily to their constant danger from the persecutors, although this factor undoubtedly kept them on the move. It has been well established by now that the Great Commission was fundamental to their thinking, and this at a time when the state-church Reformers not only ignored but denied the relevance of this dimension of the Word.[21] Moreover, in spite of generations of pilgrimage during which no real missionary work was possible, the Mennonites—as Professor Pannabecker has concluded in his study of missions in the General Conference[22]—showed a peculiar responsiveness to the claims of the Great Commission when it was again laid on the churches in the nineteenth century. In the earliest period, the Hutterites mounted the most effective program of missions; in Menno's writings, however, we also find constant emphasis on that aspect of Christian witness. Mark 16:16 and Matthew 28:19 are used again and again as the texts to anchor the argument.

"The greatest of all emperors, Christ Jesus, . . . has all power in heaven and on earth. . . ."[23] To proclaim that truth is to deny the limitations of tribal or racial religion. Menno's knowledge of the new voyages and discoveries was more limited than that of the Swiss Brethren, who at one point thought of going "to the red Indians over the seas,"[24] but he did ask why men should oppose the Holy Spirit, who quickens all kinds of people—Frisians, Dutchmen, Germans or Walloons, Jews and Gentiles.[25] The Word, as Menno understood it, was a universal/Catholic/ecumenical force, not a parochial or provincial spirit.

The references to the Great Commission in Menno are integrated into two aspects of an active faith. In the first place there is the sense that the Word has a sending power. The Christians are a pilgrim people. The church is "cut loose from the world." In contrast with Christendom's style and limitations, the Gospel is both to and for all creatures—in Hans Hut's phrase, the *evangelion aller creaturen* (Mark 16:15). The Word is not bound—to the tribal limitations of Western Europe groupings in the sixteenth century, to *das deutsche Volkswesen* of the Third Reich, to "the American way of life" or "southern way of life" in the American "spirit of the times" *(cosmos)*.

But after it had all been accomplished according to the Scriptures, and had been made new in Christ, He did not then send out the scribes and Pharisees with Moses' law, but His disciples with His own doctrine, saying: Go ye into all the world and preach the gospel to every creature, teaching them to observe all things whatsoever I have commanded you.[26]

In the second sense, Menno used the Great Commission to demonstrate the plain intent of the Lord as to the nature of

baptism. With it he began and concluded his basic discussion
of "the teaching of Jesus" in the book, *Christian Baptism*
(1535).[27] Baptism comes after the birth of faith, and seals the
new man in the covenant. It is the "door into the sheep stall."
Only those who have reached the age of understanding can
properly be held accountable. Today, with our deeper understanding of the importance of the transition from childhood
through puberty to mature self-consciousness, we can better
appreciate the startling significance of this proposition. The
children are secure in Christ's sacrifice until such time as they
shall have reached the age of discretion. When we remember
that up until little over a century ago, in many so-called civil-
ized countries, children of seven, eight, and ten were being
tried and hanged as responsible individuals for any one of a
long list of crimes, we begin to see the revolutionary significance of the Anabaptist principle. The occasion of the pro-
nouncement on children was profoundly religious, but the
benefits to mankind were in the long run profoundly temporal
as well.

Most beloved, since the ordinance of Jesus Christ is unchangeable,
and is the only one that counts with the Father; and since He has
commanded that we shall first preach the Gospel, and then baptize
those who believe, it follows that all those who baptize and are baptized without the teaching of the Gospel, and without faith, baptize
and are baptized on their own opinion, without the doctrine and the
ordinance of Jesus Christ.[28]

With God there is no respect of persons—emperor, king,
Ph.D., peasant, and craftsman are all alike before His counte-
nance.[29] Here again there was a radical universality to Menno's thinking, shared by other Anabaptist leaders. They were
massively critical of those who held the positions of power
and control in this world's darkness, as—indeed—the Bible is
also.

For ye see your calling, brethren, how that not many wise men
after the flesh, not many mighty, not many noble, are called:
But God hath chosen the foolish things of the world to confound

the wise; and God hath chosen the weak things of the world to confound the things which are mighty;

And base things of the world, and things which are despised, hath God chosen, yea, and things which are not, to bring to nought things that are:

That no flesh should glory in his presence (I Cor. 1:26-29).

Nothing aroused Menno's wrath more than the hypocrisy of sycophants and hangers-on, as is amply evident in his *Reply to Gellius Faber* (1554).

> *In the third place Gellius has dedicated his writing to a nobleman, as is customary with the learned ones; thinking perhaps that by this means their aim will be more easily attained, through the favor and support of such dignitaries; a thing which the pious witnesses, prophets, and teachers, especially of the New Testament, never desired and much less sought or employed concerning God's truth and Word.*

He is a hireling, moreover, one who has hired himself out, as a servant at certain wages and a stipend, contrary to the example of Christ and the example of all the true messengers who have been sent by Him.

But for what purpose Gellius and all the preachers of the world are called may be determined from their doctrine and work; namely, to preach as the magistrates and the world like it.

Also, observe here his hypocrisy and his harmful flirtation with the great, for where do we find, alas, more ungodliness than among those in authority?[30]

It would be a mistake to think of Menno as a social revolutionary, any more than Amos and Hosea belong in that category because they condemned them that trod upon the poor, lay upon beds of ivory, laid house to house and field to field, and by their wickedness invoked grasshoppers for the crops and blasting for the land. Nevertheless, not all magistrates were capable of making that distinction between incendiaries and Anabaptists, since the latter were just as obviously sympathetic to the poor peasants and craftsmen as they were determined to dissociate themselves from their mistaken use of violence.

18

Also my poor brother, whom he so hatefully brings up, did no greater wrong than that he erroneously, alas, defended his faith with his fists and met the violence committed, just as all the learned ones, preachers, priests, monks, and all the world do.[31]

Those who criticize the violence of the poor of Münster should realize that all war and violence is wrong and not just that of the oppressed! According to Menno, those who oppressed the poor, persecuted the righteous, and disgraced the Lord were themselves guilty of sedition.[32]

The living Word was, then, for all men of all stations of life—with the active presumption that those who heard the Gospel gladly at the time of Jesus would again respond more readily than the high and the mighty. Within the church, moreover, class differences were abolished. We have forgotten, now, what the situation was in the churches when separate sittings were introduced for men and women.

The state-church chapels of old Europe can refresh our memory; Catholic and Protestant, they have booths for king or lord of the manor, reserved pews for persons of station, standing room or back benches for the common folk. When men and women were seated separately, and when in a *Bibelstunde* a simple lay farmer might instruct magistrate and merchant, a mighty step forward was taken in the fixing of the independence of the church and her standards. The people shaped by the impact of the Word of God became a model of human relations to the world, a "city set on a hill," even though the world as such continues in the main to resist the example set.

The living Word was the Word of salvation through Jesus Christ, of the continuing work of God the Holy Spirit in His church. The mood or atmosphere in which the Word moved was one of hope and promise. Unlike an arithmetical table or new code of the law—as though the Gospel were but a law of Christ which had taken the place of the law of Moses—the Word of God was ever speaking, ever renewing, ever perfecting, ever creating new men and new women for the time to come. The joy must remain constant, the hymns of discipleship never stilled!

O worthy men, check yourselves and ponder the matter. Consider the end and ponder the outcome. You rely on human invention, but we on the Word and truth of God; you rely on the world, we on heaven; you rely on the present, we on the future; you rely on the emperor and force, we on Christ and His promises, until we all appear before Him who will come in the clouds of heaven to requite all flesh. Then you will see what you have lived for, what office you filled, what deeds you have done, for what hire you served, whose word you promoted, whose counsel you despised, and whom, O men, you have so hatefully stabbed.[33]

Whether the Word renewed or condemned, then, depended upon the response or posture of the listener. We do not find in Menno the inexorable decrees and irresistible election of a certain type of Protestant orthodoxy. His thought was fundamentally evangelical: the initiative of the divine Word calls for, demands of men, a responsive and joyful witness. In this, Menno's theology of the Word is in harmony with the great accent on evangelism and mission which has, beginning with the Great Century of the expansion of Christianity, shifted the center of the faith from European Christendom to the younger churches—the Free Churches of America, Africa, Asia, and the islands of the sea.

There remains the final query whether Menno identified the literal, textural word with the Word of God, as though the terms were interchangeable, the bounds of each the same. It seems to me significant that whereas a whole generation of Lutherans was to be distraught by debates about the Hebrew vowel points, Menno and the Anabaptists avoided such peril. To be sure, "the whole Bible must be understood and interpreted in the light of Jesus Christ," as Dr. Waltner has put it; but I am not, however, so persuaded of the following statement, that ". . . their interpretation of the Scriptures was Christocentric while that of the reformers was theocentric . . ."[34] This requires more discussion.

The Christian life, and all Christian thought of the Bible record, began indeed with the sacrifice and resurrection of Jesus Christ. But beyond that, the Anabaptists seem to me to have rediscovered a principle which was also operative in the early church, in the attitude to and use of the canon. Both the "Keys of Peter," to loose and to bind (church discipline), and the "Key of David," which unlocked Scripture, belong to the congregation. They were not only protected thereby from the errors of the Reformed, "with their ahistorical conception of Scripture as a monolithic body of authoritative revelation."[35] They were also protected from the error of the Spiritualizers, who reduced both Scriptures and sacramental order to a minor rank after individual insight and conscience.[36]

I would like to propose that here, too, a unique contribution of the Anabaptists was the understanding of the work of the Holy Spirit. At the present time this is one of the most needed emphases in general Protestant thinking: as Henry P. Van Dusen has pointed out, the mission fields and much of American religious life are filling up with various inspirationist sects and cults. Their teaching on the Spirit is frequently individualistic and schismatic. The fault, however, lies with those churches which never developed an adequate and lively proclamation of the works of the Spirit. Menno's theology provided such.

We have then the person and work of Jesus Christ pivotal in all understanding of Holy Scripture, but in addition the action of God the Holy Spirit in making the Word intelligible and related to the life of the awakened readers. The Bible was opened in the meeting of fellowship and then laid upon the life of the church. It was not something which each individual could read and interpret as he pleased. In Anabaptism, as Paul Peachey has emphasized, ". . . salvation is of necessity corporate."[37] The Bible was read and related to the life of the Christian people in that context, in that setting. This was not the Catholic position, i.e., that "the church must be the lord of Scripture because the church made the Scrip-

21

ture."[38] Rather the Word disciplined and shaped the church and the church opened and proclaimed the Word, by the power of the Spirit.

CHAPTER II

Menno and the
True Church

During the twentieth century the Christian people have
been confronted by pseudo religions of appalling intensity.
Nazism and communism, as variant forms of totalitarianism,
have claimed more martyrs and swept away more sections of
Christendom than any hostile faith since the rise of Islam a
thousand years ago. It has been during this engagement that
theologians in Europe have begun to question the whole
orientation of nineteenth century culture-religion and doubt
the usefulness or validity of values and principles apart from
the life of a witnessing community. Indeed, one of the most
sturdy leaders of spiritual resistance in the Lutheran church
of Bavaria has summed up his lessons learned during this
period with these words:

The Christian should never verbalize a position which he is un-
prepared to make a matter of witness.

"Idealism" is no longer the key word: the stress is now on
"witness." Reinold von Thadden, lay head of the Kirchentag,
the great rally of the church in Europe, has referred to that
movement as "the end of Protestant individualism." The concern for the church has replaced individual emancipation in
the new movements. In the lay movements which have
emerged from the period of the church struggle many of the
basic questions being discussed are of the kind that we might
call "pre-Anabaptist." That is, they step outside the old context of Protestant culture-religion to rethink and rework the

23

doctrines and practical disciplines of the *ecclesia motans* (1945 Kirchentag), *ecclesia viatorum* (1959 Kirchentag).[1]

Behind all this there is the new conviction that only when the Word is made flesh in a disciplined people is a real force at work, that history is in truth carried by a believing community rather than disembodied ideas. Here the immediate relevance of the Anabaptist-Mennonite witness is apparent. For in the sixteenth century the concept of the church as a community disciplined in mind and conduct according to New Testament standards was represented almost alone by the Anabaptists. In a direct way they strove to restore the true church as it had been before the "fall," before the pride of the hierarchs, the arrogance of the professional theologians, and the ambitions of temporal rulers had enhanced its outward show of prestige and weakened its true inward strength.[2]

The church of the New Testament era was normative. "Apostolicity" meant to be "true to the apostles," not to be standing in a long unbroken line of clerical ordinations. In this sense the Anabaptist view of the church was directed toward the past, toward a norm which had once flourished but had been defaced by compromise. But the restored church walked just as truly in the light cast by things to come. As John Wenger has stressed, in *Separated unto God*, the true Christian community has a prophetic mission.[3] The view of the true church in the past is also the vision of the true church of the future.

In an age where pressure from the "younger churches" is raising anew the question of the life and style of the New Testament church, the classical Anabaptist witness is especially relevant. The astonishing thing is that a scholar like Karl Barth can raise the questions—without once realizing that men died for the same thing in the sixteenth century, and that a statesman like Hendrik Kraemer can discuss the apostolate of the laity—without once referring to the churches which once went through the fiery furnace to maintain the possibility of lay initiative at congregational level!

24

In Menno's thought there is a sure rule by which the true church can be identified: "namely, where the Spirit, Word, sacraments, and life of Christ are found. . . ." These are certain sure signs by which the church is distinguished, and these were listed succinctly in the *Reply to Gellius Faber* (1554):

1. . . . the salutary and unadulterated doctrine of His holy and divine Word.

2. . . . the right and Scriptural use of the sacraments of Christ, namely, . . . baptism . . . the Lord's Holy Supper. . . .

3. The third sign is obedience to the holy Word, or the pious, Christian life which is of God.

4. The fourth sign is the sincere and unfeigned love of one's neighbor.

5. The fifth sign is that the name, will, Word, and ordinance of Christ are confidently confessed in the face of all cruelty, tyranny, tumult, fire, sword, and violence of the world, and sustained unto the end.

6. The sixth sign is the pressing cross of Christ, which is borne for the sake of His testimony and Word.[4]

In short, to the emphasis of Luther upon Word and sacrament, Menno added four other signs which remind us of the old evangelical virtues: obedience, love, nonresistance, suffering. Theology was not enough: holiness of life nourished the fruits of the spirit.[5] He warned against the antinomian tendencies already apparent in Lutheranism and later to cause the most acute internal conflicts within that movement.[6] That the magistrates were led to cruelty and the people to immorality raised serious doubts as to the true orthodoxy of their churches.

With Calvinism, a later formulation of Christian priorities, the case was different. There is now a considerable body of evidence that Calvin's *tertior nota,* the "third mark of the church," was itself derived from encounter with the Anabaptist witness in Hesse and Strassburg. At least Calvin added his extensive treatment of church discipline, in the *Ecclesiasti-*

cal Ordinances of November, 1541, on returning to Geneva from his period of exile in Strassburg (1538-41). It was precisely at this time that Butzer had his conspicuous success in winning over sections of the Hessian Anabaptists, a success which was achieved by introducing the use of the ban at the Ziegenhain Synod of the Hessian state church.

Butzer had agreed that church discipline was Scriptural during the Marburg Disputation of 1538 with the Anabaptist elders, and Philipp of Hesse ordered his preachers to add the ban to the church order when he became convinced that at this point the Anabaptists had the Gospel on their side.[7] But in addition to Word, sacrament and church discipline (which is not mentioned in Menno's list, although implicit there and frequently expanded elsewhere), Menno added other marks of the true church.

Menno's discussion of Christian baptism was based on the interest to restore the primitive meaning, the meaning in use before whole populations were baptized by coercion and numbers of infants by habit. Infant baptism was condemned as "anti-Christian," and evidence was introduced from the church fathers to show baptism was directed at adults until unscriptural ceremonies became common. The use of godfathers and sponsors was also late and an innovation.[8] Both in the book on *Christian Baptism* (1539) and in the long section against infant baptism in the *Reply to Gellius Faber* (1554),[9] the words of the Great Commission are featured as words of institution.

Menno's understanding cannot be seen solely in terms of his relation to the high teachings of the reformers. It was also shaped by conflict with the spiritualizers. His basic statement is clear enough.

. . . baptism is a sign of obedience, commanded of Christ, by which we testify when we receive it that we believe the Word of the Lord, that we repent of our former life and conduct, that we desire to rise with Christ unto a new life, and that we believe in the forgiveness of sins through Jesus Christ.[10]

We must see that he was standing over against the spiritualizing thrust as much as against the materialistic view on the other side. This is the answer to the puzzle put in a recent article by Vincent Harding,[11] as to why Menno sometimes listed the act of baptism before salvation and sometimes after. The New Testament ordinance and the conditions for it were inexorably interrelated for those who had heard and understood what Christ intended.

In presenting the doctrine of the Lord's Supper, he wrote both constructively and defensively. He opposed the materialistic interpretation of the elements, but was unwilling to "burden the good and pious reader with quarrelsome, fruitless disputing concerning the outward sign, as do the learned ones. . . ."[12] He was particularly strong in use of the Scriptural injunctions as to when the meal ought to be eaten and when it would do hurt to the participant.

Oh, delightful assembly and Christian marriage feast, where no gluttonous eating and drinking are practiced, nor the wicked vanity of pipes and drums is heard; but where the hungry consciences are fed with the heavenly bread of the divine Word, with the wine of the Holy Ghost, and where the peaceful, joyous souls sing and play before the Lord.[13]

In a beautiful passage he adopted the language of the *Didache* to describe the essential communion fellowship:

Just as natural bread is made of many grains, pulverized by the mill, kneaded with water, and baked by the heat of the fire, so is the church of Christ made up of true believers, broken in their hearts with the mill of the divine Word, baptized with the water of the Holy Ghost, and with the fire of pure, unfeigned love made into one body. Just as there is harmony and peace in the body and all its members, and just as each member naturally performs its function to promote the benefit of the whole body, so it also becomes the true and living members of the body of Christ to be one: one heart, one mind, and one soul. Not contentious, not spiteful and envious, not cruel and hateful, not quarrelsome and disputatious one toward another like the ambitious, covetous, and the proud of this world. But in all things, one toward another, long-suffering, friendly, peaceable, ever ready in true Christian love to serve one's neighbor in all things possible: by exhortation, by reproof, by comforting, by assisting, by counseling, with deed and with possessions, yes, with bitter and hard labor, with body and life, ready to forgive one another as Christ forgives and serves us with His Word, life, and death.[14]

Here are summed up the final qualities of the true church, created by the Word and sustained by the means of grace: obedience, brotherhood-love, suffering, and discipline. All of these qualities were apostolic, and all belonged to the church of the restitution. All pointed toward the time of fulfillment.

When we perceive the dynamic work of God the Holy Spirit in the church we are saved from a static view of virtues which might otherwise be legalistic and moralistic. For Menno the Word is ever creative and recreative, and the people of God are being perfected toward the end in the kingdom.

"In short, with these people old things have passed away—"[15]

These people are the people of the resurrection, being made new men and new women.

This resurrection includes the new creature, the spiritual birth and sanctification, without which no one shall see the Lord.[16]

Anabaptism is neither institutional nor propositional, and it is this which above all differentiates it in the end from Roman Catholicism and Protestant scholasticism.

Anabaptism rests ultimately on perpetual spiritual re-creation which derives its authority from the work of the Spirit among men thereby united, and not from ecclesiastical structure.[17]

This dimension and atmosphere of life lived in expectation of the kingdom, this confidence in a God who works yet among His people, is vivid in Menno. Without it, he or his people might have sunk into the kind of sterile restorationism which later characterized one wing of the Campbellite movement. The restitution is never a finished task, but must be undertaken again and again.

The regenerate, therefore, lead a penitent and new life, for they are renewed in Christ and have received a new heart and spirit. Once they were earthly-minded, now heavenly; once they were carnal, now spiritual; once they were unrighteous, now righteous; once they were evil, now good, and they live no longer after the old corrupted nature of the first earthly Adam, but after the new upright nature of the new and heavenly Adam, Christ Jesus, even as Paul says: Nevertheless, I live; yet not I, but Christ liveth in me. Their poor, weak life they daily renew more and more. . . .[18]

Menno's grasp of the sweep of God's revelation in the Old and New Covenants is exceptionally vivid; indeed, the very sense of history, its past and its impending fruition, kept his strong moral and ethical sense from descending to banality and complacency. The strong disciplines maintained were ever in anticipation of time to come. He challenged the churches:

If ye are the true Christians, where are your Christian ordinances of baptism, Supper, diaconate, ban, and Christian life, as commanded in His Word? If ye are the truly baptized ones of Christ, where is your faith, your new birth, your death unto sin, your irreproachable life, your good conscience, your Christian body into which you were baptized, and your Christ whom you have put on?
O beloved brethren, men have erred long enough.[19]

Jesus Christ, who is the present head of the church—against the claims of popes, lay bishops, theologians, and town councils—is the same before whom in time to come every head shall bow.

And there was given him dominion and glory, and a kingdom, that all people, nations, and languages should serve him.[20]

Neither was the style of Anabaptism propositional; the recent charge of a Roman Catholic scholar that Lutheranism fell into this error, substituting not a book for a pope but a dogma for both, cannot be brought against Menno. The claim is that Luther taught not only that man must be justified by faith, but that he must believe in the proposition of justification by faith.[21] Whether this is a fair charge against Luther,

29

it is assuredly a fair charge against some who adopted the position of Lutherans. Even among contemporary exponents of Lutheranism belief on justification by faith, and that interpreted in a certain way, has become a kind of fixed point in a universe otherwise in flux. For example, in an article appearing in the current issue of *Church History* the Anabaptists are charged with failure to make justification by faith central to their system of thought, and all of the old charges and misunderstandings of their ethical and moral correctness are dredged up and presented anew as though more than a generation of serious research had never dented four centuries of polemics and misrepresentation. Near the close we find the conclusion,

But instinctively—or theologically—the Reformers saw that on the Anabaptist system man was given once more an important place. Their violent reaction is understandable.[22]

Thus again is the Anabaptist distinction between the lostness of the natural man and the discovered potential of the new man in Christ ignored, and decades of brutal and anti-Christian persecution glossed over—and all because the thinking of the radical Reformers did not fit itself solely to the central proposition of a certain view of theological orthodoxy!

For Menno, as for Grebel and Marpeck and Hutter, "orthodoxy" did not consist alone in an intellectual proposition. The tests of a vital orthodoxy included the good fruits which are brought forth by a good tree. More than that, devotion to a certain style of life distinct from the "spirit of the times" was one mark of Christians in fellowship with Christ and each other. This principle of discontinuity, of separation, was the real offense which the political and religious leaders of Christendom could not bear. And in those days, before the coming of the "post-Christian era" in Europe, they had fire, water, and the sword to enforce the measure of their displeasure. Today, there is nothing left but the repetition of old and exploded calumnies and the ignoring of primary sources.

It is not enough that we say, we are Abraham's children, that is, that we are known as Christians.[23]

O beloved reader, our weapons are not swords and spears, but patience, silence, and hope, and the Word of God.

So Menno wrote, in *The Reply to False Accusations* (1552).[24]

With the restitution of the true church there comes naturally the kind of persecution that the early church endured before the leaders of the institution apostatized and accommodated to the world. Here again the emphasis is placed on the saving remnant which redeems the times and, indeed, carries history.

It continues as it was from the beginning when there were but four persons on the earth of whom the Scriptures testify that two were disobedient and a third slew his brother. There were eight righteous ones when the world was drowned and one of them mocked his father. In Sodom and Gomorrah with the adjacent country, there were four righteous persons; one looked back and was changed into a pillar of salt. More than six hundred thousand valiant men left Egypt and only two of them entered the promised land. Not, dear Lord, that all were damned who died on the way, but they did not on account of their unbelief inherit the promised Canaan. So now also, dear Lord, is the eternal land promised to us all if we walk in the way which Thou hast chosen for us. But now they walk the crooked way of death, and therefore, even as those did not inherit the temporal, so will also these not inherit the eternal Canaan.[25]

There is a permanent tension between the Word and the world which approved of itself and will not change.

And I say that the unprofitable and rebellious world is commonly warned and rebuked against its will, so that the majority of the prophets and the true servants of God are condemned and killed by the princes and magistrates as seditious mutinists, and persecuted by the priests and common people as deceivers and heretics.[26]

But more terrible than the winnowing of the faithful in antiquity, and more to be condemned than the persecution of the early church by the heathen, is the apostasy of the so-called Christians who themselves refuse to obey the Word and then put to death those who do.

31

It is a frightful abomination and raging terror thus miserably to garrote, to kill, and wipe out those who with such ardent hearts seek the Lord and eternal life, and who would not touch a hair of anyone upon the earth.[27]

Who are the persecutors?—

. . . an unbelieving, carnal, earthly, wanton, blind, hardened, lying, idolatrous, perverted, malicious, cruel, unmerciful, frightful, and murderous people, who by their actions and fruits show that they neither know Christ nor His Father, even though they so highly praise His holy name with their mouth and extol it with their lips.[28]

By persecuting the faithful the rulers of Christendom prove themselves to be under the brand of Antichrist, in a role far more terrible than the condition of early non-Christian enemies of the faith. In weakness and suffering the true church continues under the sign of the covenant, living in anticipation of the kingdom which is to come.

The Anabaptists, and those who followed after them, are sometimes accused of dissolving the ministry, since they have condemned those who held high office in Christendom as priests, theologians, and canon-lawyers ("Roman doctors").[29]

O reader, precious reader, it is a fearful thing to fall into the hands of the living God.[30]

Menno wrote very plainly about those who preached for hire and held their commissions from town council or prince rather than the church of God.

I say again, Inasmuch as your preachers are hired and bought at a stipulated salary or wage, and do not preach unless they are hired, they must acknowledge that they are hirelings, and not teachers that are sent; for they do not teach by the compulsion of the Spirit and love. . . .[31]

The calling of the servants of the Word was to the service of the church. Servants of the Word there were, and among the Hutterites stewards of economic affairs as well (Diener der Notdurft). But theirs was a "representative ministry": the accent was placed upon the ministry of the whole people of God. As Harold Bender put it in writing on "The Call to the Ministry"—

When it becomes necessary to fill the office of deacon, with which also the proclamation of the Word was connected, the Twelve did not simply impose a man selected by their power upon the church but they called the church together (Acts 6:2-6) and said ". . . Brethren, look ye out among you seven men of honest report, full of the Holy Ghost and wisdom, whom we may appoint over this business." . . . Hence, every man is susceptible to the call of the church if he is living according to the church. All men of the church are to be prepared for this high calling. All should have a Christian witness, therefore a Christian ministry.[32]

All Christian men have a ministry: this is the conviction which the newer lay movements in Europe, such as the Kirchentag and Evangelical Academies, are trying to recover after more than four hundred years of the practical denial of the vaunted slogan, "the priesthood of all believers." At the time when it was first enunciated, those who took it seriously and tried to organize themselves accordingly were rebuked openly by the Reformers for not keeping the common folk in their proper place. Rather than eliminating the ministry, as has sometimes been charged to the Anabaptist and radical Puritan account, they eliminated the laity of the sort known for centuries. The docile, silent, obedient subjects of lay bishops and hierarchs were replaced by a witnessing, ministering people. This was the church as a community of disciples, as *bekennende Kirche* in the age of the Reformation.

Finally, we must consider the way in which Menno viewed the words of God in the light of the promises to the church. With all of his stressing of moral and ethical uprightness, Menno never claimed that he or his brethren had attained Christian perfection. Rather was "church" an eschatological concept. The nature and style of the Free Church were known, and even in incompleteness those who lived by the future contrasted strikingly with the prevailing state of culture-religion. But Menno never claimed that they had attained to the goal, in spite of accusations that he was introducing a "new monasticism" or new "legalism."

You will see that we are grounded on the only eternal cornerstone, and walk, albeit in weakness, in the right way, and have the plain truth, and that there is no other way or truth to be found in the Scriptures that can stand before God, other than this which we have pointed out. . . .

This is my only joy and heart's desire: to extend the kingdom of God, reveal the truth, reprove sin, teach righteousness, feed hungry souls with the Word of the Lord, lead the straying sheep into the right path, and gain many souls to the Lord through His Spirit, power, and grace. So would I carry on in my weakness. . . .[33]

Here is no perfectionism, but rather the *motif* of the Pilgrim Church, the *ecclesia viatorum*. It is the mood and atmosphere of a church which lives by the covenant, is disciplined in this life, looks to the daybreak of the kingdom across generations and nations, lives in expectation that God will do greater works through His disciples than He did even on earth in the flesh. A true church is perfect only in weakness, in being obedient to God's purpose for her in this imperfect and dying world. In the final sense, perfection lies in the future—at that point where church and kingdom become one, at the end of history, when the lordship of Jesus Christ is re-established over all the worlds that He has made.

To the shaping up of the Christians, church discipline is indispensable. Church discipline seems from the outside to consist chiefly of negatives, with the ban its chief method and means. To be sure, Menno wrote much on excommunication, expulsion, and shunning, and not always felicitously. He warned rightly against a city "without walls and gates."[34]

. . . This binding key of Christ is given to His ministers and people so that they by it may declare in the power of His spirit to all earthly, carnal, obdurate, and impenitent hearts their great sins, unrighteousness, blindness, and wickedness, as well as God's wrath, judgment, punishment, hell, and everlasting death and so crush before God, terrify, humble, pulverize, and make them sorrowful, distressed, sad of heart, and small in their own eyes. Wherefore it is compared in its power and virtues to the rod of the oppressor, a hard hammer, the north wind, a sorrowful singing, and with a pure, cleansing wine.

Over against this the key of loosing is given to the end that with it the ministers and people of God may direct such contrite, troubled, dejected, sorrowful, sad, and broken hearts (which are enabled by the former key to feel and see the deep mortal wounds and sores through the spiritual brazen serpent) to the throne of grace; to the open fountain of David; to the merciful, compassionate High Priest, our only and eternal sacrifice of atonement, Christ Jesus; and so heal the sores and stripes, and the venomous wound of the hellish serpent. Therefore it is compared in pertinency to the cheering olive branch of Noah's dove; to the balm of Gilead, to the voice of the turtle dove, to the south wind, the joyful pipe, the sweet-smelling ointment.[35]

Looking back on it, Menno's experience with the ban was not one of the brighter aspects of his ministry. Yet we must appreciate the historical situation. He and his colleagues were making one of the first advances in the restitution of voluntary discipline in the church, among a class of people where illiteracy was high, tribal loyalties intense, and where the massed pressures of established church and state were striving to penetrate and destroy the movement. Apostasy was a serious business for leaders with prices on their heads.

Menno lived for nineteen years under an imperial edict which offered pardon to any common criminal who would deliver him up. When members left the congregations, under duress or through falling away, they became an immediate threat to the life and limb of those who remained faithful. Under these circumstances it is no wonder that Menno and Bouwens and others had difficulty in defining the practical implications of a discipline which plainly rested on New Testament instructions, but which under religious persecution carried political and legal significance as well.

To the member of the church, however, the ban was only the outer limits of church discipline—rarely exercised, and seldom present in his consciousness. On expulsion as an ordinance he wrote:

I repeat. We have used the faithful service of our brotherly love from our inmost hearts; we have admonished and entreated them, and have put up with some of them a whole year or two, ever waiting and hoping the best of them, and have not hastily separated them. . . .[36]

The real nature of church discipline was not the corrective phase, necessary as it might be at times: the essential matter was brotherhood-love. Meeting to read the Bible and for common prayer, studying the temptations and possibilities of the common life for witness, admonishing and exhorting and upholding, the simple Christians worked out their salvation in fear and trembling, rarely conscious that the structure of church discipline calls—in extremity—for purging the reprobate as well as encouraging the regenerate. Thus the restored church fulfilled her Lord's purpose, perfect in the power of her hope, though weak and defenseless in this world.

CHAPTER III

Menno and the Doctrine of the Laity

No subject is discussed more excitedly in ecumenical church circles today than the doctrine of the laity in the church. During the church struggle with Nazism, the established churches in the former center of Christendom discovered the great price which may have to be paid if the significance of the layman's vocation is neglected. Today the phrase used to describe the mass of silent and drifting constituents is as harsh as that applied by the Anabaptists in the sixteenth century: *getauftes Heidentum.* At the special synod of the Evangelical Church in Germany called in June of 1956, a leader of the struggle with Nazi—who is currently the most vocal Christian opponent of communist totalitarianism in East Germany—expressed convictions that might have been lifted bodily from an Anabaptist document:

The situation of Christianity in contemporary Europe is now characterized by alert minds by the saying that the end of the Constantinian era is at hand.

The Barmen Articles, in which in the name of the sole lordship of Jesus Christ all hyphenated Christianity is repudiated, remain significant as the charter of the freeing of the Biblical Gospel from a Babylonian captivity.

The Constantinian union marked the end of the common way of the church of Jesus Christ, a way which according to the view of the New Testament will be one of agony before the contradiction and resistance of the world.

After the end of the illusions about the Constantinian age, and in return to the early Christian witness, we do not have the right to

37

demand from the state privileges and monopoly for the support of the Gospel.[1]

To this Menno could only say "Amen!" The astonishing thing is that in all this rediscovery of the church as the whole *Laos tou Theou,* in this talk about *ecclesia viatorum, Kerngemeinde, Kirchenzucht,* and the "apostolate of the laity," there is as yet no realization that this has all been said before and said very well. The first lay movement of that type in northern Europe was main-line Anabaptism. Only the constant repetition of the many times exploded calumny that the genius of Anabaptism was revealed in the Peasant Revolt and at Münster, and the failure of many church historians and theologians to check the facts by the primary sources, can explain this unwillingness to give the *Täufer* their due.

When we turn to the Anabaptists, we find the new periodization of church history already well developed. Whereas the Protestant state churches, until the rise of Pietism and Puritanism, held like the Catholics to the historical scheme of Augustine and Orosius—in which the Christian church centered the next to the last age of church history, in unbroken line from the *Acts of the Apostles* to the Last Judgment, the Anabaptists introduced and popularized the typology Gunter Jacob is here using: early church, "fall" and restitution. The restitution was a return to the genius and style of life of the early church. Basic to the restitution was the end of the "Pastorenkirche," against which Reinold von Thadden of the Kirchentag inveighs: the true church should emerge again as the community of disciples sharing a common ministry.

One of the most profitable ways to review church history is to study it in the perspective of the layman, the "forgotten man" of church history. Such a systematic study has not yet been made, although the time is at hand. Since August of 1957 an international group of church historians has been preparing a book on *The Laity in Historic Perspective,* to parallel the work of H. Richard Niebuhr on *The Ministry in Historical Perspective* (Harpers, 1956). The situation is quite simply this: with the exception of recent studies published by French Dominicans, and the volume by Hendrik Kraemer, this is a neglected area of Christian theology and historiography. Church history is still largely taught as the history of popes, emperors, Christian princes and town councilors, with theologians thrown in for seasoning. The latter are there not because they shape events but because they write the books!

When we survey church history from this point of view we perceive entire landscapes neglected by previous explorers of the past. The study of the laity confirms the periodization earlier noted. In the early church the Gospel was spread by laymen. As with Islam throughout its history, the claims of the religion were put forward by ordinary craftsmen, traders, travelers. With Constantine, as Congar has noted in *Lay People in the Church* (1957), the laity lost out. Several of the "leading laymen" of the early church were troublesome anyhow—Marcion, Tertullian, Priscillian, Pelagius—and from Nicaea on it was the emperors who took whatever initiative laymen exercised.

With the exception of monasticism, originally a lay movement, there were no channels for lay devotion open to the ordinary communicants. With the sixteenth century we have the reassertion of lay initiative: certainly much of the power behind the Reformation was due to the unwillingness of the rising commercial and national ruling classes to be relegated any longer to the role of spectators in the liturgy and planning of the Christian life. But in the Protestant state churches the theme was suppressed, due to the determination of Lutherans, Calvinists and Strassburgers to hold on to the medieval parish system of counting communicants. Lay initiative emerged, and it was the initiative of Christian princes and town councilors—not of the whole church membership. When Duke John of Saxony or Landgraf Philipp of Hesse or Jacob Sturm of Strassburg instructed their subjects in religious matters, they expected as ready obedience as in political or military affairs.

Here was the rub of the controversy between the church of the Reformation and the church of the Restitution. In my judgment it was more serious in most cases than any doctrinal differences, since we still dispute to this day whether the Lutherans of the Augsburg Confession (1530) take the Bible more seriously or the Anabaptist-Mennonites, whether the Calvinists of France and Scotland took public responsibility more seriously or the radical Puritans.

For the Anabaptists the authority of the magistrate stopped at the door of the church: matters of faith were reserved for the governance of God the Holy Spirit in the congregation. For the state-church Reformers, religion was one dimension of a continuum still called "Christendom," and subjects were expected to obey with docility and silence in confessional matters as well as political.

Of course, as long as Zwingli and Calvin, Luther and Melanchthon lived, the magistrates tended to act under the impress of advice from the preachers and theologians. But, as Roger Ley—a Swiss scholar—has pointed out in *Kirchenzucht bei Zwingli*,[2] as soon as the great generation died out, the worst evils of the caesaropapism against which the Anabaptists had warned began to take effect.

Menno's words are plain enough:

I would say further, If the magistracy rightly understood Christ and His kingdom, they would in my opinion rather choose death than to meddle with their worldly power and sword in spiritual matters which are reserved not to the judgment of man but to the judgment of the great and Almighty God alone. But they are taught by those who have the care of their souls that they may proscribe, imprison, torture, and slay those who are not obedient to their doctrine, as may, alas, be seen in many different cities and countries.[3]

The history of religious liberty and the recovery of the role of the laity begin, in fact, at the same point in church history: at the point where the headship of Jesus Christ and govern-

40

ance of God the Holy Spirit in the church were practically asserted, if need be by acceptance of the baptism of blood.

It was the integrity of the church as a community of witness under her true Head which made men rebuke the presumption of the princes to rule there, too, by virtue of their status in the world. It was the same integrity of witness which required that all of those baptized in the faith—and not just those with technical education—should pray, discuss, and determine the shape of Christian witness in the world. Religious liberty was not enunciated first as a civic virtue but as a matter of Christian obedience. The apostolate of the laity was not put forward first as a means of supporting the institutional program or raising money for promotion: it was essential to the restitution of the true church.

The charges brought against the Anabaptists show the truth of this assertion, even apart from the plain evidence of the internal sources. The preachers of Zurich rebuked the Swiss Brethren for holding unauthorized meetings in homes to study and expound the Scriptures. For generations the Swiss cantons forbade preaching or teaching except by license of the town councils. The rule in Strassburg and other imperial cities was substantially the same. In the states of central and north Germany the princes controlled appointments and maintained that "whoever preaches without authorization is an enthusiast."

When the brethren justified their actions by the texts of the Great Commission and the first verse of Psalm 24, the state-church theologians declared that lay people should stay in their proper stations in life; the Great Commission had in any case been exhausted in the apostolic age and was no longer operative. This whole point has been discussed on another occasion at considerable length.[4] But the implications in so far as lay initiative was concerned, or what is now called "the role of the nonprofessional missionary in spreading the Christian faith," are amply clear.

Equally important in the long course of church history is the place given by the Anabaptists to laymen in the work of witness at the level of the congregation. Even our use here of the term "laymen" reveals the degree to which we still make the old and false distinction between ordained and unordained classes. In the New Testament *Laos* and *Kleros* are simply different ways of referring to the whole people and a shared responsibility. In Anabaptism there began that discussion which now excites attention, as to the ministry of the whole people by virtue of their ordination in Christian baptism. This is precisely what Menno meant by baptism, by an understanding start in the covenanted life.

We do not read in Scripture that the apostles baptized a single believer while he was asleep.[5]

Thus he answered those who played down personal responsibility in order that infant baptism might be retained. In dying again and being raised in Christ by believers' baptism, they of the covenant were sealed in a ministry—a "group ministry," if you will. The disciplinary standards for such congregations of ministers were in important respects higher in fact than those which bound the clergy of the state churches. The pronounced opposition to a paid clergy[6] was also part of the drive to prevent separation of the whole community of witness into classes, as well as to secure the liberty of preaching against patronage. When the ministry of rebuke is to be exercised, "It shall be done by the congregation of God,"[7] a position which ran into some difficulty when Leonhart Bouwens acted arbitrarily in his office as bishop.

When the education of the children is considered, borne up as they are by the sacrifice of Christ until such time as they have reached the age of understanding, their parents' responsibility is to teach them to read and write and to learn a useful craft; but above all they are to learn the fear of God,[8] looking toward such time as they shall come into mature service as Christians. All of these matters were discussed in the context of the role of the whole witnessing and ministering people.

Menno was insistent upon lay literacy far in advance of his

age, so far as the common folk were concerned, because only a membership able to read and discuss the Bible could serve in the church. His intense feeling about recantation and apostasy was as much as anything due to the fact that such was betrayal of the high calling of the ministry: he was as exercised about an ordinary member's falling away as the state churches were about the loss of a priest or theologian.

But here again the positive aspect of the fellowship must be brought to the fore: the glory of life in Christ was the joy of witness. He could not sympathize with, and was deeply critical of, those who separated the assurance of justification from the lively witness to the love of Christ toward all His creatures. His indignation at the Reformed preachers who betrayed the hidden congregation after the Mennonites had brought them food and clothing across the ice when their ship was stranded in winter derived from the fact that they had met Christian *diakonia* with treachery.

Then, as now, the Mennonites were known for their service to victims of famine, flood, and the plague.[9] Then, as now, it was a witness of a whole people—not the marginal service of those with special interest in such things, and not a "Bishop's Fund" administered by a high officer alone.

When we consider the development of the Free Churches, there was another dimension to the Anabaptist-Mennonite style of churchmanship which compels respect. Long before the western world claimed to honor and respect the dignity of the common man, he was known and loved in these congregations.

The Anabaptist-Mennonites were no social revolutionaries; yet there was a whole new style of human relations in the congregations of the Anabaptists and those who followed after. At the door of the church the power of the secular prince halted. This was the beginning of religious liberty. At the door of the church the claims of class privilege halted. This was the beginning of a new style of human relations, in which for the first time in centuries in the relations between human beings—also in the church—men attempted to see the least brother through the eyes of Christ rather than according to his status in the world.

For generations after the Reformation the state churches accorded in their ranks the deference to lord bishops, princes, councilors, and personages of social status the titles and obeisance which were theirs in the kingdom of this world. In Anabaptist circles, even with noblemen and ladies, rank was calculated according to the gifts of the Spirit. And none was of such humble station but he was called "brother," and his concerns and words honored like those of all others. All were members of one body of disciples, and they had assumed a liability both spiritual and practical for each other. Although only the Hutterites organized a communism of production, all branches practiced a fellowship of sharing.

Beloved reader, it is not customary that an intelligent person clothes and cares for one part of his body and leaves the rest destitute and naked.[10]

We have here what today is called a "group ministry," with the most practical measures of mutual aid within and the most vigorous standards of Christian service to the needy outside the fold. In the *diakonia* as in the *kerygmatic* function, the natural self-assertion of the individual was yoked and disciplined to mold and express a collective witness to the honor of the Name.

Today we find a good deal of free use of the phrase, "the priesthood of all believers." Occasionally a careful writer in the Lutheran or Anglican tradition will point out that there is a general priesthood but not all are called to the "office" of the ministry. In fact, "the priesthood of all believers" is meaningless unless there are specific structural provisions whereby it may be exercised. It may be that on occasion, influenced by the prevailing pattern in Christendom, Mennonites, too, have distinguished too sharply between those called to a special function and those who carry the general ministry of the faithful. If so, this is questionable Anabaptist-Mennonite procedure. For the special ministry is a functional, a representative ministry in the New Testament; it can only be seen properly against the background of the ministry of all baptized believers.[11]

Anabaptism provided some of the structures whereby the general ministry could function. The Lutherans, and to a lesser degree the Calvinists, asserted the principle of a general ministry, but in practice held the common layman in his place. Even in New England, where Puritanism had its best opportunity to develop for a time an unmixed pattern of lay initiative and general ministry, the leaders of Plymouth and the Bay Colony reverted to the old class structures within the church. Pews were allotted according to social position. Tax money was used—in Connecticut until 1819 and in Massachusetts until 1834—for the support of the clergy and instruction in orthodox religion.

Those who attempted to constitute an unlicensed and voluntary expression of religion were harried out of the land, and some were put to death. In the classical period of Anabaptism, however, congregational order, congregational worship, family structure, missionary endeavor, social service and relief were so ordered as to provide an opportunity for the whole membership to share in the ministry.

————————

What is the "office" of the general ministry? For if the ministry is not to be limited to a special class, with a special and exclusive "office," some thinking must be done at this point. Neither the state churches nor the Free Churches have to date come up with very satisfactory answers to this question.

Nowhere is the distance between the sixteenth century and the twentieth century greater than in the daily life of the ordinary communicant or lay member. The little congregations which Menno shepherded consisted of people now largely anonymous—simple peasants, craftsmen, and tradesmen, in the main. So far as social structures were involved, life was still close to agriculture and the world of nature. It had not changed substantially since the time of our Lord, either in pace or in style. The chief daily witness of the Christians was expressed in neighborly virtues: kindness, charity, mutual aid, probity in business dealings, avoidance of quarrelsomeness, gossip, and brawling.

In Lutheranism the ethics of vocation/*Beruf* were developed, but the feudal and agrarian bent led to its being interpreted in conservative terms: peasants, guild members, princes, and professors were to remain in their stations in life. For practical purposes, instructions as to one's role in society were given only to the rulers.

The Calvinist system and thought-world have been shown to be particularly attractive to the rising commercial classes—not so much because Christian instruction was provided as because certain medieval restrictions were removed. The chief accomplishment of Calvinism, beginning with William of Orange's introduction of military drill and continuing through Cromwell's New Model Army, may have been in articulating the soldierly ethos.

Otherwise, with the exception of those groups which have preserved a certain type of Christian agrarian life and philosophy by following the frontiers, a unique witness or style of life for Christians was not cultivated. And now even that which we retain in certain reserved areas of society is beginning to weaken. Or, at best, it has narrowed down to a certain kind of individualism—in which a quality of individual and family life is still maintained in spite of the pressures of the world.

But even this individualism is subject to the gravest pressures in the modern world of rapid communication, incessant stimuli, mass media. What is the future of Christian community witness if our discontinuity, our principle of separation, is lost? What will the next generation be like if, as is rumored, half the farm houses in Lancaster County are surmounted by TV aerials? What kind of people will we be when we live in air-conditioned rooms, cut off from the sounds and smells of nature? What will our souls be like after years under constant artificial light? What is happening to us under the constant stimulus of forced listening—taped programs on buses, in hotel rooms, in restaurants? Is there no solution but to move to the Primavera [communal colony in Paraguay], to seek out the lost frontiers where a sober and hard-working agrarian ethic can be maintained? For what will happen even to rural Mexico and South America when, as we are told, the population bomb has exploded to seven billion persons by the year 2000?

In answering these questions, so different from anything our fathers could have imagined, we are facing one of the gravest crises in the history of the faith. It took until 1830 for the world's population to reach one billion. A century later it had doubled. From 1930 to 1960 a third billion were added. At the present rate a fourth billion will be added in little more than a decade. At this rate, all places of refuge will soon be gone and the farming which is done will all be "industrial farming."

In the U.S.A., where the shift is still going on apace in the Southeast and Southwest, the movement from agrarian life to the metropolis has been accomplished within the lifetime of our own parents. In 1890 over 80 per cent of the American people lived on farms or in rural villages; today the figure is approximately 10 per cent.

What is to be our response to this new situation, with demographic experts predicting that by 1980 there will be a solid city (megalopolis) from Wadsworth to Findlay, Ohio; from Arlington, Virginia, to Melrose, Massachusetts; from Toledo, Ohio, to Lansing, Michigan? "Die Welt," to use the title of a splendid little book by Eberhard Mueller of Bad Boll on the "apostolate of the laity," "ist anders geworden." How can the life and ministry of the regular members be so supported and shaped in the life of the church that this utterly new situation can be faced with joy and faith and not by the romantic idealization of an age gone by—in religion or in politics?

Here, too, the life of the church is at stake. And we must face frankly the fact that the Anabaptist-Mennonite ecclesiol-

47

ogy is more directly vulnerable than many others—for example, the Roman Catholic or Lutheran, where the doctrine of the church is so readily spiritualized and internalized. If the true church is a redeemed, visible, disciplined, witnessing community of disciples, its mission and encounter with the world are quite different from that of "the church in the heart." The alternative is quite plainly "evangelize or die." As to priorities, priorities in line with the genius of the Anabaptist-Mennonite heritage, I would like to suggest three points of attack.

In the first place, and here the fathers' faith and practice can be of profound assistance to us, we must consider what the effect of constant mass stimuli is upon the personality. The inevitable result, for the natural man of intelligence and sensitivity, is withdrawal in upon himself. There is no need now to discuss those who simply accept and absorb all the stimuli like a blotter: they will become the Gammas of Huxley's *Brave New World*. Because he is the object of constant, blaring, and raucous pressures from radio, TV, or forced listening on buses and restaurants, the intelligent man retreats behind a mask and strives to defend that little domain of privacy left to him from all invasion. The problem is that in doing so he loses the capacity to respond, to communicate, at points where creative action is needed. His self-created world of the sound-proofed chamber, the one-way eyeglasses, becomes a prison.

Some months ago Norman Cousins of *The Saturday Review* published an editorial on a representative incident. It occurred in the waiting station of a commuters' railroad to New York. As all were standing about, each in his own world in orbit toward the office in the city, two young delinquents suddenly entered and beat to the floor a man who had been standing there among the commuters. And in all this none of the gray-suited spectators, even after the initial shock, lifted a hand to help him. Cousins' editorial, or sermon, was to ask what kind of organized life was producing that indifference.

The reports from the Korean campaign, where thousands of

American soldiers were simply abandoned along the roadside to die, is another case in point. In the modern world of high organization and high pressure, dehumanization is already far advanced.

The life of fellowship, of alternating separation and service, can save us from the fate of the Gammas and the fate of the spectators. Separation must be maintained, else we become robots. This is simply another way of saying what our fathers taught, that the church—in which we attain to our true humanity as God purposed it to be—saves us from violation, destruction, and death of the soul. The "means of grace"—frequent fellowship, common prayer, communion, Bible study hour—are quite literally the medicine of the soul. By identification with the blessed community we are preserved from spiritual death.

The Head of the church is "the joy of the disconsolate."[12] The life of the natural man is isolation, the lostness, the atrophied response to others. In spite of the considerable attention given to the ban, to the life of persecution, the consolation of the life of faith and hope breaks through in Menno again and again. We are healed in fellowship. And it is this which makes it possible for the church to school us to be selective with our separation and our mission. We shall need the church even more desperately than did our fathers, who lived closer to the face of growing things, as the times approach their climax.

Second, in the development of the megalopolis the inner city is being neglected.[13] The Protestant churches have followed the middle class into the suburbs and are abandoning the "people of the dirt" to whom the Gospel was good news, release, sight, "the acceptable year of the Lord." More recently the Roman Catholics, too, have begun to desert the inner city. This means that the majority of America's people, some 67 per cent of them, who still inhabit the waste places from which leadership has taken flight, are left to the tender mercies of Jehovah's Witnesses, fly-by-night tent and tabernacle artists, "I Am" and other mystery religion and gnostic cults.

49

The most significant work in this neglected area is that of East Harlem Protestant Parish, Cleveland Inner-City Parish, and the related work in New Haven, Boston, Detroit, and Chicago. This new style of endeavor, experimental and imperfect though it is, is a group ministry under discipline. There is much that is hard and repelling about the life which such ministers and their families must lead; food and clothing are austere, housing is poor, street life is often violent and always distractive, the church meetinghouses are store-fronts and rented halls.

It seems to me that, as strange as it sounds in an address to a people that has been traditionally rural in orientation, the inner city is precisely the area which calls for the kind of community witness for which the sons and daughters of Menno are justly noted. In the world which we are moving toward, for some time to come the group witness to purity of life, Scriptural simplicity, nonviolence, sharing, spiritual government, the "house church" as a community of brethren, etc., will be desperately needed. For generations the Mennonites have moved into the desert places and through faithfulness, mutual aid, and plain hard work turned prairies and jungles into garden places. What would be the impact if the Mennonites would tackle the most desperate deserts and jungles of America, the inner cities from which the prevailing forms of culture-religion are fleeing?

The question cannot be answered in prudential or sociological terms. But I do not know that true Anabaptists have ever looked at an area in need of witness and service with a canny calculation as to the immediate statistical potential. Rather have they committed themselves and their work into the hands of Him who rules the affairs of nations and generations and is mightily able to perform miracles at the very places where the wisdom of this world denies a redemptive possibility.

Finally, I believe that we can benefit from a more energetic cultivation of the "trans-Atlantic dialogue." The Free Churches in America are the bridge between a dying Christendom and the younger churches, and they must face toward Europe —in this new role—as well as toward the mission fields. The relationship can be of great mutual benefit. On the one side, it would be difficult to exaggerate the importance of the work of the Mennonite Central Committee in the broken Europe of the postwar period.

The European Christian minorities have expressed again and again their gratitude for relief and reconstruction, and above all for the spirit of forgiveness and reconciliation with which MCC personnel has carried the witness of Christian fraternity. They need and want the "Apostolat de la Présence" now, as much as earlier they needed material assistance. Those who are asking what I have called "pre-Anabaptist questions" need fraternal workers to help them to find a new way in the ruins of Christendom.

In Africa and Asia the witness of the fraternal worker and "nonprofessional missionary" is welcome, even in areas where the official missionary is no longer tolerated. In short, the situation calls for precisely that style of total church witness, of lay ministry and initiative, which was so central in the Anabaptist-Mennonite restitution of the true church.

On the other side, the Reformation emphasis upon the doctrine of vocation/*Beruf* is being recast in contemporary ecumenical thought, without the feudal bias which was so much a part of sixteenth century state-church teaching on the subject. In agrarian society, community is a matter of geographical proximity. In the industrial age, community is primarily vocational or professional. Surgeons, dairy farmers, wheat farmers, steel workers, barbers, lawyers, personnel managers, and even historians have their basic norms of daily ethical and moral conduct shaped by the nature of their trade associations.

What is a Christian dairy farmer? What is a Christian wheat rancher? Can a Christian be a soldier? If the classical Mennonite doctrine is still supported by a negative consensus at this point, let us ask another: Can a Christian be a physicist?

51

Can a Christian be an advertising expert? If so, where does he draw the line? Quite evidently most Protestant ethics, and not Mennonite alone, is still largely rural in its mind-set. But there are whole sections of modern life totally unevangelized, in which prevailing practice is little above the ethics of the jungle.

In the early church, and in the Restitution, the principle was stated that Christians were "better than the laws" in their conduct. What is the witness today on this point? The lay movements which have been striving to rebuild professional ethics and morals in Europe, after the corrosion of Nazism, have discovered some few things which could help us better to point up the ministry of the laity in the world. Here, too, the Mennonite concept of witness by the whole people of God—rather than isolated individuals—affords a spiritual power for good that can bring a testimony at the right place at the right time.

All of this, when we fix our eyes on the enormous political and social and economic problems, seems hopeless. But when our minds are lighted by the mind of Christ, and by remembrance of God's purpose for a suffering humanity, we recall that with Him all things are possible. As Menno put it again and again, "The power of the Spirit and the Gospel truth in Christ Jesus"[14] will yet triumph over all persecution, all opposition, all hazards of this life.

CHAPTER IV

Menno and the Doctrine of the Holy Spirit

In his elaboration of the doctrine of the second person of the Trinity, Menno was not always well directed. Although the Swiss Brethren never followed him in his Christology, and the Dutch Mennonites soon dropped that line of thought, we cannot deny that flaw in his teaching. He admitted that he hated to dispute the issue, and would have been better guided not to do so and simply hold to his expressed conviction that "it is an exalted and incomprehensible miracle of the Almighty and great God."[1] In brief, his purpose was to emphasize the heavenly flesh of Christ and the glory of His person, and in doing so he denied the Chalcedonian formula of the two persons.

He was assisted in this lapse by the primitive state of scientific knowledge in that day as to the role of the female in reproduction.[1] But we must remember, too, that he was opposing in mortal spiritual combat three major denials of the majesty of our Lord: 1) the error of the Catholics and others who asserted the church itself to be the body of Christ, in a spiritual continuum with the actual, physical body, and with mediating grace lodged in and limited by the elements in the Mass; 2) the error of the visionaries and religious revolutionaries who claimed the presence and authority of the indwelling Word to justify their views or programs; 3) the error of the book-worshipers, who suppressed the living Word by devotion to the text of that which was written.

In the area of Christology, Menno sometimes used expressions, to safeguard the divinity of Christ, which were inept and pointed toward difficulty rather than edification. For example, he referred to Christ in phrases reminiscent of the old Docetic view that the Christ, of the same substance as God, was never truly incarnate, but he never accepted the denial of the true humanity of Christ, which he asserted repeatedly.

He did not become flesh of Mary, but in Mary.

. . . as an apple is called the fruit of a tree . . .[3]

In *The Gospel of Thomas*, a Gnostic text discovered recently at Chenobaskion, we find a form of words not unlike this:

. . . like water through a pipe so He passed through the virgin Mary, receiving nothing from her and not being changed.[4]

It has been commonly assumed that at this point Menno simply followed Melchior Hofmann's Christology. And since his brethren refused to follow him, and their descendants have had no desire to accent Menno's fault by discussing so patent an error, rarely has someone bothered to ask whether Menno's Christology was in fact consistently Docetic or even to determine what intention lay back of the infelicitous choice of words.

Unlike the Gnostics, Menno was anything but anti-historical. He was not moved by a desire to repudiate the temporal sphere and to enunciate timeless truths. On the contrary, he was plainly moved to stress the divinity of Christ in opposition to vulgar expressions of incarnational teaching. He was confronted, and he was convinced that the faith was mortally threatened, by teachings which were in fact powerful if unwitting expressions of the ancient Monophysite heresy.

The first of these with which he had to deal was the identification of a human community with the power and flesh of Christ: this was the heresy of the Roman Church which, during the years of his Christian ministry, was being canonically defined by those sections of Christendom which remained obedient to the Bishop of Rome (at the Council of Trent, 1545-63). This institution claimed to be an extension of the power and flesh of Christ, and as such endowed with godlike authority and immunity from criticism. In becoming a committed and active Christian, Menno left the priesthood of the Latin Church and became a wandering preacher and bishop, gathering up the scattered faithful into the baptism of the New Covenant. There never left him thereafter the certainty that the pattern of the true church was set in heaven and laid out in the New Testament, and that no human institution could rightly claim to be in a continuum with the divine.

Menno remained constant in the conviction that God's purpose was expressed in chastening and judgment, in continual correction, in "the Protestant principle." Secondly, Menno confronted the challenge of the Münsterites, who also identified an earthly city with the heavenly plan. As he strove to gather up those who had been disheartened and broken by another crude identification of Christ's power and person with a person and community other than those authorized by the New Testament, his denunciation of John of Leiden and his colleagues was powerful and consistent.

Finally, he confronted in many of the privileged Protestant bodies a type of Bibliolatry which also confused the divine with a human artifact—the printed canon. He readily perceived that the Word of God, the divine Logos, was not to be identified with the texts translated by Jerome or Martin Luther. The richness of his understanding of the truth contained in the doctrine of the Holy Spirit, in which only Martin Butzer equaled him among the great Reformers, prevented his slipping into a faulty form of words in regard to the third person of the Trinity. But in expressing the power and authority and majesty of the second person his choice of words was less happy.

Instead of perceiving immediately and maintaining consistently that the answer to a false continuum of Christ and culture is a true incarnational doctrine, a persuasive presentation of the authority of the Word who was made flesh, he tended to stress the distance, the removal, the distinction between the heavenly flesh and human flesh of Christ. If he slipped occasionally into heretical language in so doing, he was opposing a far greater heresy in it; the heresy of Roman Catholicism, of the Jehovah's Witnesses, of the book worshipers—who have forgotten that He can, if He will, raise up children of Abraham from the very stones of the earth and grant His grace and spirit to a new elect bearing fruits more worthy of repentance. Menno's so-called "Docetism" did not stem from uncertainty of identification of the first person of the Trinity as the God of Abraham, Isaac and Jacob. The truth is that he was reacting to false incarnational theories, to blasphemy. But he asserted to the full the humanity of Christ, with no trace of Docetism.

Which of these views, asked Menno in presenting the heavenly person, accords Christ the highest honor? This was his preoccupation, to open the path that He might pass through those who sought to lay hands upon Him.

I say that He is not flesh as they have it, but that the regenerate are flesh of His flesh as the Scripture says.[5]

His intention was so to honor and elevate the Lord that the crudely materialistic abuses and misuses of His person would be corrected or at least kept out of his own flock. For this reason, too, Menno never identified the indwelling Word with the second person of the Trinity, and thereby his followers were long spared descent into the kind of subjective Jesus-mysticism which has marred much of latter-day Protestantism.

For Menno, and for the Anabaptists generally, the Word was the Gospel *about* Jesus Christ. (The religion of Jesus, to which liberalism and Pietism have appealed, was, of course, Judaism.) The word about Jesus Christ and the living Word which converts were never deliberately separated in Anabaptist thought. Wiswedel summarized the situation very aptly in discussing the inner and outer Word:

"The case is this: the Anabaptists, seeing that the new preachers were giving disproportionate emphasis to the written Word of God and that the masses by their consent to the printed and proclaimed

Word had not become new creatures, on their part then stressed the 'inner Word,' occasionally disproportionately too, but not to the extent that they removed the Spirit from the written and preached Word; otherwise they would, of course, not have everywhere appointed and chosen preachers of the Word *(Diener des Worts).*[6]

It may be this reserve toward God in Jesus Christ and hearty affirmation of the work of the Holy Spirit which affords a chief ground for the distinction between Anabaptism and Pietism, a most important distinction which Robert Friedmann's classical work[7] has permanently fixed in our memory. It may well be, too, that the poverty of much Protestant thought in the matter of the Holy Spirit is responsible for the fact that so much of the religious poetry and writing of nineteenth century culture-religion has indulged in a sentimentalism about Jesus which is often no less vulgar than the cruder forms of Mariolatry.

After all, according to the Bible and the classical Christian confessions, He ascended into heaven and when next we see Him face to face He will come in the terrible role of Judge, not as a lover in a garden. And God active, sending, governing, chastening—whom we know as the Comforter, the Spirit of Truth, who dwelleth in the midst—is God as Holy Spirit. Menno was very clear on this, and it may be, too, that the very fact that his doctrine of the second person limped helped to save him from the more common error in Protestantism: an atrophied and unsatisfactory doctrine of the Holy Spirit. God is able to turn even our weakness and stumbling to His greater glory and honor!

Nowhere among the figures of the sixteenth century Reformation or Restitution do we find a richer doctrine of the third person of the Trinity, God the Holy Spirit, than in Menno Simons. This richness of understanding, with a significance for church government which I have discussed at length on another occasion,[8] showed itself in many different ways in his writings. It averted certain problems on the relation of the inner and outer Word, as the Wiswedel quotation implies. It maintained the historical and eschatological perspective, and helped to ward off both sterile scholasticism and religious subjectivism. Neither a crude literalism nor a timeless "spirituality" is indigenous to Anabaptism.

The belief in "belief" which is so characteristic of contemporary American piety will find no sustenance in Menno's writings, nor in those of his peers in other wings of the Anabaptism movement. Neither will the assertion of some internal "experience," which is presented without the objective validation of an historical revelation, satisfy.

In Anabaptism, the ground of our faith is an event which occurred and occurs again in a moment of time. The center of our faith does not consist of sets of theological propositions demanding our assent, nor of emotional compulsions which express themselves in the semi-erotic language of latter-day "spirituality"; these are sub-Christian or at best pre-Christian. With Anabaptism, the center of initiative remains with God—not with the inward workings of human intelligence or the human soul.

The Bible is full of examples of true faith among those "who beheld the promises from afar off" and those who knew the presence of Him who was sent: Noah, Abraham, Moses, Joshua, and Caleb, King Josiah, the centurion of Capernaum, Zacchaeus, the thief on the cross, the woman who sinned, the Syrophoenician woman, and so on. The Word which was laid from the foundation of the world has been working among a remnant, a vanguard, a faithful folk from the beginning. The Word was never the dead letter of a law, and He may not be bound by the letter of a new legalism—of precept or of proposition or of authority of office.

Oh, that God might grant that the blind watchmen of this world, I mean the preachers and the scribes, might pitch their pipes to the right tune . . . ![19]

Menno blamed the state-church preachers and theologians for the persecution and abuse of the defenseless Christians. And it was they who, by divorcing right doctrine *(reine Lehre)* from the life of Christian love, encouraged the secular rulers in cruelty from which simple humanity might have restrained them.[10] The princes, regents, and lords are deceived by the preachers,[11] who do not call them to repentance[12] but rather allow them to join doctrinal rectitude with moral corruption and unjust rule. The way of faith cannot be separated from the way of the witnessing community; intellectual confession and orthodoxy must be matched by orthodoxy of life. Prophets and seers of the Old Testament, as well as the whole burden of the New Covenant, are agreed in this.

The canon is closed, but the history described in the Bible, the providential works of God, are by no means finished. Menno steered another course from that which led to the formation of the Roman Catholic Church at the Council of Trent (1543-65), with all power and authority concentrated in an institution. He avoided the error of Protestant scholasticism, which until it met the dissolving force of the Enlightenment— or in some sections nineteenth-century critical scholarship— identified the text of the written word with the Word of God and enthroned a new Sanhedrin interpreting a new casuistry.

As Harold Bender has stressed, in the Anabaptist-Mennonite line the Bible can never become a new table of the law, a new weight like a cement block.

. . . its chief value is as a redemptive book; it is the Book of life.[13]

The peculiar style of controversial writing in the sixteenth century, in which proof-texting was a general practice among all parties, can mislead us at this point unless we remember Menno's truly astonishing willingness to discuss and to trust the power of the Holy Spirit to give new light. We err if we suppose this openness to encounter was merely formal, a kind of diplomatic preface to intellectual tourney.

What was involved was another process of articulating and applying truth from that indigenous to Roman Catholicism or state-church Protestantism. And it was also different, because checked by both Bible and church, from the inspirationism of some of the contemporary sect movements which recently have been called a "third force" in Latin American missions.

The Word proclaimed was to be checked in the meeting. The Lutheran emphasis led to a certain self-justifying process in preaching, with consequent indifference to reception or response. There are still sections of conservative Lutheranism where missionary—as well as social—witness is condemned: the Christian responsibility is limited to the preaching of the Word and the sacramental order. After World War I some younger preachers in Berlin and in the Baltics introduced the "talk-back session" after the Sunday morning service, to the profound gratification of students and young laymen who had been used to having an orthodox sermon laid out with no contact to their lives. The orthodox, however, were shocked and complaining: the self-evident nature of the Word was called in question. After World War II, at the first international laymen's conference (Bossey, 1948), the leaders gathered said quite bluntly that the problems they now had could not be solved by sermons; only real discussion (*Gespräch*) could help. The laymen in the European state churches are still struggling, in short, with a system which has never understood rightly that the Word becomes a true Word at the moment of communication . . . at the point when the outer Word makes contact with life. Recently the head of the pioneer lay center at Bad Boll, Dr. Eberhard Mueller, stated that —although a Lutheran theologian—he had now come to the conviction that another mark must be added to *Wort* and *Sakrament*, namely, *Gespräch*. For it had pleased God in the fullness of time to bring us to the point where lay people themselves must be involved in the discussion and process of defining the Christian witness: they are no longer willing simply to be told, to take orders.

Anabaptism had from the beginning a different style of laymen, and a different theology of the Word. The locus of the living Word was not in an office (*Amt*) but in the congregation. In conservative Anabaptist-Mennonite and radical Puritan circles to this day a wide variety of methods may be employed until the outer Word, corrected by the Spirit, becomes the Word written on the hearts of the faithful. There may be preaching by one or by several; there may be silence and waiting for wisdom or there may be exhortation or group singing; there may be single short statements or active discussion of a troubled point. The preacher may even stop and ask those present to question, or correct, or confirm—for the final end of all preaching is the edification of the church and the enlargement of her witness, not the enhancing of the preacher's reputation as logician or orator. Here we see again how in Anabaptism the special minister is chaplain to the lay folk, who carry the faith, who are in the world witnessing. In all of this, however, it is God the Holy Spirit who prepares the ears to hear and the hearts for understanding. It is He who confirms and gives concrete authority and relevance to that which has been read out or spoken.

Nor was it only in the church among brethren that Menno was confident of the value of open-faced discussion, of fearless confrontation. He repeatedly pledged obedience to the ruler where he was competent, and begged to be instructed according to the Bible in case of religious error. He denied that his insistence upon openness of discussion was incitement to rebellion.

Therefore I say, if you find in me or in my teaching which is the Word of God, or among those who are taught by me or by my colleagues any thievery, murder, perjury, sedition, rebellion, or any other criminal act, as were and are found among the corrupt sects —then punish all of us. We would be deserving of punishment if this were the case. I repeat, if we are disobedient to God in regard to religious matters, we are willing to be instructed and corrected by the Word of God, for we seek diligently to do and fulfill His most holy will. Or if we are disobedient to the emperors in matters to which he is called and ordained of God, I say matters to which he is called, then we will willingly submit to such punishment as you may see fit to inflict upon us. But if we sincerely fear and seek our Lord and God, as I trust we do, and if we are obedient unto the emperor to temporal matters as we should be according to the Word of God (Matt. 22:21; Rom. 13:7; I Pet. 2:13; Titus 3:1), and if then we have to suffer and be persecuted and crucified for the sake of the truth of the Lord, then we should consider that the disciple is not above his Master. . . .[14]

The basic elements in Menno's teaching on church and state stand forth clearly here, and show him to be a true pioneer of the Free Church position.

1. The government is to be obeyed in temporal matters.
2. The competence of the government does not extend over matters of religious faith and practice.
3. A good government does not persecute those who are being true to the Word of God.
4. If there is error of religious belief it should be corrected in brotherly fashion by proof from the Word of God, and not by sword.

All of these points set Anabaptism off from state-church Protestantism. Zwingli took it for granted that the cantonal government should control the religious faith and practices of their subjects, as well as other public matters. Luther agreed to a pattern of control which passed the power and decision in religious matters to princes and town councilors.

The leaders of the Anglican break from Rome were above all determined to reserve to the monarch the right of appointment, of initiative and decision in the religious affiliations of his subjects. And, although Catholicism theoretically retained authority in matters of faith and morals and church order in the hands of the church, in point of fact the emperor and Roman Catholic princes held on to a large measure of control through to the beginning of the nineteenth century. In Menno's time the major confessional bodies, with some modifications in Strassburg and Geneva, were all parochial and particularistic and controlled by patrons. Menno and his people stood for a larger measure of integrity and universal perspective than any other churches of the time.

. . . we are asked to attach ourselves to the princes and the learned ones if we do not want to be tortured or burned at their hands, or be murdered by some other tyrannical means. As if the preachers were sent by the princes rather than by Christ![15]

Menno's goal was not to establish a Free Church as such, or to improve society by eliminating the old curses of ecclesiastical cabal in political affairs or political intervention in spiritual matters. His goal was the restitution of the New Testament church. But from this there sprang secondary benefits which pointed toward a purer church and a better style of government, both.

Most striking is Menno's confidence in the discipline of the fellowship. He was willing that they should all stand accountable for each other, not only before the face of God but to the civil authorities as well. This derived from his certainty that their standards of belief and behavior were based on consensus rather than coercion. He knew that, unlike the large proportion of "fellow travelers" and "rice Christians" which betrays the state churches in adversity, his brethren could be counted upon. They were baptized into the covenant on profession of faith having reached the age of understanding and wittingly accepted the burdens of membership.

More important yet, in terms of their loyalty and "we-feeling" toward the movement, they had been enlisted through common prayer and discussion in the general priesthood of believers. They were not in spiritual matters the subjects of a hierarchy or civic prince advised by professional theologians and canon lawyers: they were, so to speak, fully franchised citizens of the kingdom.

Thus, although Menno's political vision never reached beyond the late medieval responsibilities of a loyal subject to an absolutist liege lord, in his church view he moved far beyond the structures and behavior patterns of a static Christendom. One hundred years later, in radical Puritanism, the lessons learned about human relations based on consensus in the congregations of the faithful were to reach out into the political sphere and bring a new and "democratic" style to town meeting as well as church meeting.

63

Menno came back frequently to insist on his openness to full and open discussion. In 1552 he wrote four tracts to plead for the cessation of the persecution of his people, and offered to debate publicly ten basic questions if given safe conduct. His offer, made in his "Brief Defense to All Theologians" (1552), was not accepted,[16] though he repeated it many times. In the Preface to his "Reply to False Accusations" (1552), he had urged that the proper stance for Christians was one of brotherly and face-to-face encounter.

Before God, reasonable reader, what we most sincerely desire is that with all our writing, teaching, living, misery, distress, and confiscation of our goods we may one day gain so much mercy from the children of men that we shall be allowed a private discussion with our adversaries before any number of pious, intelligent, and reasonable men who love and fear the Lord and who can distinguish between good and evil, at least if a public meeting is not allowed. Would that their lies and accusations would not be believed until teacher is confronted with teacher, and the accuser before the accused, with equal rights and liberty, as the Word of God, Christian love, and natural reason teach and imply. . . . But we fear that a hearing will not be allowed us.[17]

In an age where the tradition of persecution and suppression was so strong, Menno's view of the way to form the public mind was amazingly enlightened. Again, although it was a century later that there appeared Christians who understood the relationship of open discussion to creative politics, Menno's view clearly presaged a new standard of human relations in the body politic as well as in the church.

In his *Reply to Gellius Faber* (1554), Menno came back again to his plea for a fair hearing:

. . . I humbly beseech and faithfully admonish all my readers, friends, and enemies, to read attentively, to examine diligently, and to judge according to Scripture this my forcibly extracted reply and defense, not with the senses spoiled by partisanship, not drowsily or spitefully, but with wide-awake eyes of the soul. This matter concerns us all, namely, the praise of God and of Christ, and the salvation of our poor souls. Let none imagine that he is not included.

Why has he then twice refused a public discussion under safe conduct. . . . Which I have requested of him so urgently?[18]

I hereby offer myself to you and to the whole world, if these writings are not sufficient, and if safe conduct is granted, to an open and free discussion with Gellius and the learned ones. . . .[19]

Here he was not only setting a certain standard for decent human relations, but he was also speaking bindingly to the readers. His purpose was not to exchange opinions, nor to tickle the ears with new ideas and notions: the matters at hand were of the order of salvation, and those of other views were obliged to respond with clear agreement or disagreement. Frivolous playing with ideas was as strongly condemned as the effort to short-circuit the discussion by suppression and persecution.

Menno did not believe that such a discussion would be without objective standards—i.e., a mere diplomatic session or perhaps a "group process" ending in the lowest common denominator. On the contrary, the Bible was to be the standard by which the truth of various positions might be checked. The discussion begins and ends with the Word of God and only in that reference can it be fruitful. When he went on to write of his efforts to have a fair hearing with those who spread false rumors and inspired the rulers to persecute, he brought this out:

. . . I have long since twice requested to treat with them, on Scripture, in public, under safe conduct, before twenty or thirty witnesses or before a popular meeting. But what kind of answer I received, their handwriting, which I still possess, testifies. . . . Also, the preachers of Wesel, in the land of Cleve, made our people believe that they would furnish me safe conduct and treat with me, etc., but when I signified my willingness in writing, I received an answer that they would let the executioner treat with me, and other tyrannical and unchristian words.[20]

Menno's position in this regard was not unique among the Anabaptists. Indeed, the willingness of the restitutionists to discuss openly and accept correction when its need was proved was one of the striking things about their behavior in an age of unrelieved stubbornness and deafness of brother toward brother Christian. In 1525 the Swiss Brethren had offered themselves for a discussion.

If it be found then by divine Scripture that we err we shall gladly accept correction. We desire nothing upon earth than to have these things decided according to the Word of God.[21]

When Wilhelm Reublin and Jakob Kautz lay imprisoned in the Strassburg jail (January, 1529), the state-church preachers refused to discuss with them. They rather laid their official "refutation" of the radicals' position before the town council for action by the government. The Anabaptist prisoners replied that if they had been too summary or in error they would correct it if it were pointed out to them.

Would God that our errors would be met with the truth; how humbly we would acknowledge every wrong that occurs! But it's no use; still we ask nothing other than that we be met in this way.[22]

The Anabaptist sources are full of such expressions, and they presuppose a different understanding of the way truth is discovered and articulated from that of the Catholic or Reformers' parties. For them truth was given by the Holy Spirit, the governor of the people of God. The setting for its articulation was brotherly discussion. Truth was not defined by an ecclesiastical monarch or secular prince. Neither was it laid out by professional scribes reading and interpreting a book. It was discovered by the whole body of the faithful and represented a *consensus fidelium* when stated.

Such a principle of authority in the church is not to be confused with individualism. It was, in fact, very like the principle of conciliarism—with its emphasis on the *consensus fidelium*. More important yet, in view of the growing importance of Greek orthodoxy in America's pluralistic religious scene and in the ecumenical movement generally, the classical Free Church emphasis on the work of the Holy Spirit affords a bridge between Protestantism and Orthodoxy. The Orthodox accent on *pleroma* or *Sobornost* meets little echo in Roman Catholicism or state-church Protestantism. But in the Free Churches another spirit has been at work, one that more fully represents the old Catholic tradition and that affords a basis of conversation between the restitutionist section of Protestantism and Eastern Orthodoxy.

It is this approach which promises the mending of the seamless robe of Christ, the reunion of the churches. Submission to papal authority, assent to a dogmatic fixture from the past, reordination at the hands of a doubtful episcopacy, scarcely affords a foundation for discussion, let alone reunion. Yet we cannot rest complacently in our divisions: the re-establishment of Christian unity is also a fundamental in the restitution of the true church. Menno in his own day warned against the scandal of dividedness and the sectarian spirit, writing of

> . . . the terrible deceptions and manifold dangers in these times, there being so many and various congregations, churches, and sects all calling themselves by the name of the Lord. There are Roman Catholics or papists, Lutherans, Zwinglians, erring sects, and the Christians who are revilingly called Anabaptists.[23]

The name "Christian" or "brother" was and is enough; none of us can take pleasure in party names. But it is appropriate, particularly for a non-Mennonite, to point out that in this tradition are found the two principles most needed to effect gradual nearing of churches one to the other:

1. The centrality of the Word as the creator and governor of the church.

2. The practice of open-faced and prayerful discussion as the proper style of communication between brethren.

In the relating of the living Word to the life of the church, the Holy Spirit was called upon to guide their understanding. In common prayer, in dialogue in the meeting, the stage was set for a divine self-revelation in which the inner and outer Word made known the will of God for His people. The Word, no longer a fixum like a table or a codebook, created and shaped the witness of the faithful.

One of the most winsome passages in Menno's writing is a simple sentence in the *Reply to Sylis and Lemke* (1560), in which he admitted that he had changed his mind:

All well-minded servants of God who seek the crucified Christ and not their own honor or flesh are always ready, ever deeper to investigate the sure foundation of truth.[24]

In all honesty it must be remarked that in this case there is some reason for thinking that the particular change was not one for the better, and that he may have allowed his submission to the consensus of his fellow ministers to overweigh the Word of the Scriptures as we now understand it. Be that as it may, his willingness to be corrected is a refreshing note in an age full of self-assured and stubborn men. If His folk live in confidence that God has yet new light to break forth in His Israel, then this capacity to be corrected, to discuss and pray through decisions until a consensus is reached, is fundamental. It is in this setting of the common ministry and unlimited liability one for the other that the Christians find that the power of God the Holy Spirit also unlocks the Scriptures, making the revelation therein related not only History but our history, the admonitions therein not only of comparative significance but of compelling authority, the promises held forth not only for those who have died in the faith but for us as well.

In this moment we know that He is not only the Author of history, the Creator of all things, the final Restorer of all the tattered and broken ends of life, but that He is our God, that by His stripes we are healed, and that in His good time He purposes to give us the kingdom.

Footnotes

CHAPTER I

1. Beckmann, Joachim, ed., *Kirchliches Jahrbuch: 1949* (Gütersloh: C. Bertelsmann Verlag, 1950), p. 67.
2. Translated in full in *The German Phoenix* (New York: Doubleday & Co., 1960), Appendix B.
3. Bonhoeffer, Dietrich, *Sanctorum Communio* (Munich: Chr. Kaiser Verlag, 1954), p. 90.
4. Kraemer, Hendrik, *A Theology of the Laity* (Philadelphia: Westminster Press, 1957), p. 9.
5. Menno Simons, *The Complete Writings of . . .* (Scottdale, Pa.: Herald Press, 1956), pp. 497-98. Hereafter, *CW*.
6. *The Incarnation of Our Lord* (1550), *CW*, p. 788.
7. *CW*, p. 165.
8. *The True Christian Faith* (c. 1541), *CW*, p. 343.
9. *CW*, p. 268.
10. *Ibid.*, *CW*, p. 278.
11. *Foundation of Christian Doctrine* (1539), CW, p. 129.
12. *Christian Baptism* (1539), *CW*, p. 245.
13. *CW*, p. 49.
14. *Foundation of Christian Doctrine* (1539), *CW*, p. 216.
15. *Ibid.*, p. 220.
16. *Why I Do Not Cease Teaching and Writing* (1539), *CW*, p. 310.
17. *The Cross of the Saints* (c. 1554), *CW*, p. 586.
18. *Meditation on the Twenty-Fifth Psalm* (c. 1537), *CW*, p. 81.
19. "Exhortation to the Magistrates," in *Foundation of Christian Doctrine* (1539), *CW*, p. 192.
20. *The Spiritual Resurrection* (c. 1536), *CW*, p. 57.
21. See "The Anabaptist Theology of Missions," XXI *The Mennonite Quarterly Review* (1947) 1:5-17, and "Protestantism and the Great Commission," N.S. II *The Southwestern Journal of Theology* (1959) 1:26-42.
22. Pannabecker, S. F., *The Development of the General Conference of the Mennonite Church of North America in the American Environment;* Yale University Ph.D. Dissertation, 1944. MSS copy, p. 618.
23. *The True Christian Faith* (c. 1541), *CW*, p. 326.
24. See *The Anabaptist View of the Church* (Boston: Starr King Press, 1958), 2nd edition, p. 180, footnote 8.
25. *Christian Baptism* (1539), *CW*, p. 271.
26. *Foundation of Christian Doctrine* (1539), *CW*, p. 178. For other major references to the Great Commission, see pp. 120, 275 f., 303, 394, 513, 701.
27. *CW*, pp. 237, 242.
28. *Ibid.*, *CW*, p. 238.
29. *The Cross of the Saints* (c. 1554), *CW*, p. 585.
30. *CW*, pp. 629, 648, 649, 726.
31. *Ibid.*, p. 775.
32. *The Cross of the Saints* (c. 1554), *CW*, pp. 600, 603.
33. "To the Learned Ones," in *Foundation of Christian Doctrine* (1539), *CW*, pp. 211-12.
34. Waltner, Erland P., "The Anabaptist Conception of the Church," XXV *The Mennonite Quarterly Review* (1951) 1:5-16, 7. Hereafter, *MQR*.

35. Fast, Heinold, and Yoder, John H., "How to Deal with Anabaptists: an Unpublished Letter of Heinrich Bullinger," XXXIII *MQR* (1959) 3:83-95, 93.

36. See "Spiritualizers, Anabaptists, and the Church," XXIX *MQR* (1955) 1:34-93.

37. Peachey, Paul, "Anabaptism and Church Organization," XXX *MQR* (1956) 3:213-28, 215.

38. Bainton, Roland H., "The Bible and the Reformation," in *Five Essays on the Bible* (New York: American Council of Learned Societies, 1960), p. 21.

Chapter II

1. See "The Anabaptist Concept of the Church," in Hershberger, Guy F., ed., *The Recovery of the Anabaptist Vision* (Scottdale, Pa.: Herald Press, 1957), pp. 119-34.

2. See "The Anabaptist Doctrine of the Restitution of the True Church," XXVI *MQR* (1950) 1:33-52; also, "Christian Primitivism: A Historical Summary," XX *Encounter* (1959) 3:292-96.

3. Mennonite Publishing House, Scottdale, Pa., 1952, p. 69.

4. *CW*, pp. 739-42.

5. *Confession of the Triune God* (1550), *CW*, pp. 487 f.

6. *The True Christian Faith* (c. 1541), *CW*, p. 333.

7. See the discussion in *Landgraf Philipp und die Toleranz* (Bad Nauheim: Christian Verlag, 1957), pp. 33-34; also, Bornkamm, Heinrich, *Martin Bucers Bedeutung für die europäische Reformationsgeschichte* (Gütersloh: C. Bertelsmann Verlag, 1952), p. 17.

8. *Christian Baptism* (1539), *CW*, pp. 248.

9. *CW*, pp. 681-717.

10. *Foundation of Christian Doctrine* (1539), *CW*, p. 125.

11. Harding, Vincent G., "Menno Simons and the Role of Baptism in the Christian Life," XXXIII *MQR* (1959), 4:323-34.

12. "The Lord's Supper," in *Foundation of Christian Doctrine* (1539), *CW*, pp. 142-58; see also the section of the same title in *Reply to Gellius Faber* (1554), *CW*, pp. 717-23.

13. *Ibid.*, p. 148.

14. *Ibid.*, pp. 145-46.

15. *The Spiritual Resurrection* (c. 1536), *CW*, p. 60.

16. *Ibid.*, p. 54.

17. Peachey, Paul, *loc cit.*, p. 217.

18. *The New Birth* (c. 1537), *CW*, p. 93.

19. *Christian Baptism* (1539), *CW*, pp. 286-87.

20. *The Blasphemy of John Leiden* (1535), *CW*, p. 47.

21. Bainton, Roland H., *loc. cit.*, p. 23.

22. Hillerbrand, Hans J., "Anabaptism and the Reformation: Another Look," XXIX *Church History* (1960) 4:404-23.

23. *Foundation of Christian Doctrine* (1539), *CW*, p. 112.

24. *CW*, p. 555.

25. *Meditation on the Twenty-fifth Psalm* (c. 1537), *CW*, p. 74.

26. "To the Corrupt Sects," in *Foundation of Christian Doctrine* (1539), *CW*, p. 226.

27. *Foundation of Christian Doctrine* (1539), *CW*, p. 118.

28. *The Cross of the Saints* (c. 1554), *CW*, pp. 584-85.

29. See my article on "Ordination in the Church," in the Spring issue of *Brethren Life and Thought* (1961).

30. *Foundation of Christian Doctrine* (1539), *CW*, p. 115.

31. *Brief and Clear Confession* (1544), *CW*, p. 451.

32. Cf. Bender, Harold S., *et al.*, *The Mennonite Encyclopedia* (Scottdale, Pa.: Mennonite Publishing House, 1956-59), III, 704.

33. *Foundation of Christian Doctrine* (1539), *CW*, p. 189.

34. *Instruction on Excommunication* (1558), *CW*, p. 962.
35. *Ibid., CW*, pp. 989-90.
36. *Reply to Gellius Faber* (1554), *CW*, p. 729.

CHAPTER III

1. Cf. text and discussion in the Introduction to *Landgraf Philipp und die Toleranz* (Bad Nauheim: Christian Verlag, 1957), pp. 7-9.
2. Ley, Roger, *Kirchenzucht bei Zwingli* (Zurich: Zwingli-Verlag, 1948), p. 61.
3. *Reply to Gellius Faber* (1554), *CW*, p. 779.
4. See *The Anabaptist View of the Church* (Boston: Starr King Press, 1958), 2nd edition, chapter IV, 5; also, "The Free Church View of Missions," in Anderson, Gerald, *The Theology of Missions* (New York: Thomas Y. Crowell Co., 1961).
5. *Foundation of Christian Doctrine* (1539), *CW*, p. 126.
6. *Brief and Clear Confession* (1544), *CW*, p. 445.
7. *A Clear Account of Excommunication* (1550), *CW*, p. 469.
8. *The Nurture of Children* (c. 1557), *CW*, pp. 947 f.
9. *The Epistle to Martin Micron* (1556), *CW*, p. 920; also, see *Reply to Martin Micron* (1556), *CW*, pp. 838 ff.; *The Pastoral Letter to the Amsterdam Church* (1558), *CW*, pp. 1057-59.
10. *Reply to False Accusations* (1552), *CW*, p. 558.
11. Cf. Come, Arnold B., *Agents of Reconciliation* (Philadelphia: Westminister Press, 1960).
12. *Blasphemy of John of Leiden* (1535), *CW*, p. 36.
13. Cf. Webber, George W., *God's Colony in Man's World* (New York and Nashville: Abingdon Press, 1960).
14. *The True Christian Faith* (c. 1541), *CW*, p. 324.

Chapter IV

1. *The Incarnation of our Lord* (1554), *CW*, p. 811.
2. *CW*, p. 322; also *Brief and Clear Confession* (1544), *CW*, pp. 427 f.; *Reply to Gellius Faber* (1554), *CW*, pp. 763 f.; *The Incarnation of our Lord* (1554), *CW*, pp. 792 f.; *Reply to Martin Micron* (1556), *CW*, pp. 838 f.
3. *Brief and Clear Confession* (1544), *CW*, pp. 432, 436.
4. Grant, Robert M., *Second-Century Christianity: A Collection of Fragments* (London: SPCK, 1946), p. 133 (Valentinus).
5. *Reply to Gellius Faber* (1554), *CW*, p. 772.
6. Wiswedel, Wilhelm, "The Inner and Outer Word: A Study of the Anabaptist Doctrine of Scripture," XXVI *MQR* (1952) 3:171-91, 189.
7. Friedmann, Robert, *Mennonite Piety Through the Centuries* (Goshen, Indiana: Mennonite Historical Society, 1949), Study I.
8. "The Work of the Holy Spirit in Group Decisions," XXXIV *MQR* (1960) 2:75-96.
9. *The Cross of the Saints* (c. 1554), *CW*, p. 587.
10. *Brief Defense to the Theologians* (1552), *CW*, pp. 533 f.; also *Reply to Gellius Faber* (1554), CW, p. 634.
11. *Reply to False Accusations* (1552), *CW*, p. 554.
12. *Epistle to Martin Micron* (1556), *CW*, p. 924.
13. Bender, Harold S., *Biblical Revelation and Inspiration* (Scottdale, Pa.: Mennonite Publishing House, 1959), p. 2.
14. *Christian Baptism* (1539), *CW*, pp. 284-85.
15. *Why I Do Not Cease Teaching and Writing* (1539), *CW*, p. 298.
16. *CW*, p. 539.
17. *CW*, pp. 543-44.

18. *CW,* pp. 628, 762.
19. *CW,* p. 781.
20. *Ibid.,* p. 635.
21. Quoted in Horsch, John, *Mennonites in Europe* (Scottdale, Pa.: Mennonite Publishing House, 1942), p. 53.
22. Krebs, Manfred, and Rott, Hans Georg, eds., *Quellen zur Geschichte der Täufer, VII: Elsass, I. Teil/Stadt Strassburg 1522-1532* (Gütersloh: Gütersloher Verlagshaus Gerd Mohn, 1959), No. 167, p. 199.
23. "Exhortation to the Magistrates," in *Foundation of Christian Doctrine* (1539), *CW,* p. 190.
24. *CW,* p. 1003.